# INFINITE DEAD

# A DAILY GUIDE TO GRATEFUL DEAD CONCERT PERFORMANCES

VOLUME 1: OCTOBER

DAVID CAIN

SMALL
WHEEL
PUBLISHING

**INFINITE DEAD**
*A Daily Guide to Grateful Dead Concert Performances Volume 1: October*

ISBN  978-1-5445-2462-7  *Paperback*
978-1-5445-2461-0  *Ebook*

*Dedicated to my mom and dad*

# CONTENTS

## OCTOBER 10 . . . . . . . . . . . . . . . . . . . . . . . . .67

## OCTOBER 13 . . . . . . . . . . . . . . . . . . . . . . . . 95

## OCTOBER 14 . . . . . . . . . . . . . . . . . . . . . . . . 103

# INTRODUCTION

There was nothing like a Grateful Dead concert.

Each performance featured different songs, and every lead guitar solo was invented on the spot. You never knew what might happen next.

This improvisational approach made recordings of their concerts compelling. Every bootleg cassette tape contained mysteries dark and vast.

More than 25 years after their last performance, the universe of Grateful Dead concerts is better known. Thousands of recordings have been uploaded onto the Internet Archive's Live Music Archive, enabling fans to listen and post their comments.

But new fans and old Deadheads now face the daunting task of exploring this ocean of concert recordings and mountains of memoir. What should I listen to next? And within that two-hour concert recording, where should I begin?

How do I find the really great stuff that I still haven't heard?

In 2017, I began to listen to Grateful Dead concert recordings on a daily basis in the hope of producing a guidebook of well-researched reviews. My goal was to offer both new and veteran fans a relatively objective description of what you'd hear on the recordings.

Volume One of Infinite Dead is the beginning, featuring detailed reviews of over 200 Grateful Dead concerts performed in the month of October from 1966 through 1995.

Each concert review provides headlines and highlights, identifying brilliant musical moments sometimes overlooked by other commentators.

Some concerts are denoted with a rose. These symbols are the guide within the guide, marking your trail to must-hear music, some of which you may be well acquainted with and some you may not be.

Listening hard to the Grateful Dead every day for many years was both an enjoyable experience and a very humbling one.

As I listened to the performances—on some days across a four-decade arc—it forced me out of my comfort zone, and I found myself revising many of my preconceptions and perhaps prejudices. Or as Robert Hunter might have said, I began to look at it right.

Recorded music is forever alive, a living thing, and in each interaction with a listener something new can happen to the consciousness. The Grateful Dead's music is like the universe, in that it is infinite, and ever expanding.

The long strange trip continues…

David Cain
Marin County, California
June 2021

# OCTOBER 1

1967 Berkeley, CA, University of California, Greek Theater
(no setlist, no recording)

1969 New York City, NY, Cafe Au Go-Go
(no setlist, no recording)

1971 Santa Venetia, CA (studio)

1976 Indianapolis, IN, Market Square Arena

1977 Portland, OR, Paramount Theater

1988 Mountain View, CA, Shoreline Amphitheatre

1989 Mountain View, CA, Shoreline Amphitheatre

1994 Boston, MA, Boston Garden

## 1971 SANTA VENETIA, CA

We have two studio recordings; the second appears to include studio performances from late September. There are four songs from the 10/1/71 recording that had not been performed live (see 10/19/71 for their debuts): Tennessee Jed, Jack Straw, Mexicali Blues, and One More Saturday Night. Ripple is also here, last performed on 4/29/71 (it wouldn't see the light of day again until 9/25/80).

The other recording has Deep Elem Blues, last performed on 12/28/70. This one has plenty of piano on it (Keith's first live gig is a couple of weeks away). Promised Land has a false start (it had only been performed live five times; they'll shelve it until 5/26/72).

Other songs seemingly resuscitated only for this workout: Attics Of My Life (9/27/72 was the next one) and Mama Tried (10/19/74).

Link to recordings

## 1976 INDIANAPOLIS, IN
# MARKET SQUARE ARENA

This performance features a set two Dancin' In The Streets sandwich that wraps The Wheel, a Jam, and Ship Of Fools.

The Scarlet Begonias that comes near the end of set one is a good one. Garcia's inside solo has only two runs, but the heart-of-gold-band outro jam shines with phrases, motifs, themes, and bursts of speed (4:10–).

Set two starts with Help On The Way, Slipknot!, and Franklin's Tower (it features twelve and a half minutes of Slipknot!). After the eight-minute mark, they quiet down and cast about for a new theme, Keith's chording a distant cousin to McCoy Tyner on My Favorite Things. Lesh starts the rise (10:52) and they return to the main Slipknot! theme.

On Dancin' In The Streets, after some enticing jamming they detour into Drums for a couple of minutes then Bill and Mickey execute a nifty transition into The Wheel. The exit jam (4:02–) devolves after a minute into Weir chopping out Dancin' In The Streets, Lesh vamping on the bass, and the drummers ready to support just about anything. Garcia carries the day, veering Egyptian, but then it dissipates into, into, into…

Ship Of Fools! Perhaps the strangest segue they could find, it works beautifully, one ballad bridged to another.

Some fine work here, yet it received just two votes from Deadbase respondents in 1997 (they ranked it 32nd among the year's 41 shows). This performance deserves far more attention.

Link to recordings

### 1977 PORTLAND, OR
## PARAMOUNT THEATER

The band revives Black Peter (see 10/19/74), it will be played at least three times every year going forward through 1995.

One of the many highlights is the set-one closer Music Never Stopped. It has a relatively short mid-song break, but with some of the same lucid, phrased elements Garcia worked into his 2/3/78 masterpiece. At 6:20, he begins his furious flurry of chords—four runs worth—and instead of ending the tune, roars back into a reprise of single note soloing. The drummers supply galloping horse drums, wonderfully played.

The energy spills over into the start of set two, Bertha → Good Lovin', Bill and Mickey kicking it up at the end of Bertha. A fine example of the high-octane Fall '77 incarnation of the band.

Tonight is their 39th straight performance of Estimated Prophet (since 2/26/77), they'll finally give it a rest tomorrow night. Eyes Of The World starts with two and a half minutes of jamming before the first verse. Towards the end of the second solo, Garcia goes to all chords (7:40–), then trills them for an exciting finish (see also 2/3/78). Lesh gets a near solo at the end, though it's actually more of a quartet sound powered by Weir and the drummers (9:45–).

A smooth segue from there into Dancin' In The Streets, their sixth song pre-Drums. A great version, the early part of the jam has Garcia in a low-register grunge, the band running on all cylinders. Around 8:40, he adds a fuzzy tone.

They close strong with a great version of Around And Around.

This concert deserves wider recognition (no votes from Deadbase X respondents, though the next night here, 10/2/77, makes their top ten for the year).

Link to recordings

## 1988 MOUNTAIN VIEW, CA
## SHORELINE AMPHITHEATRE

Second of three here, Garcia's vocals are subpar in set two. The setlist highlight might be the concert-closing Uncle John's Band → Morning Dew, though the performance is underwhelming.

In set one, Friend Of The Devil, there's more of a bounce to the tempo than usual. It features an exciting transition by Garcia between his first and second solo runs, a fast run up the stairs. His voice here is OK. Queen Jane Approximately, nearly always good, has fast, pebbly runs from Garcia, and Brent's B-3 organ also gets a break.

In set two, Scarlet Begonias is a different story, as Garcia's voice sounds shaky. The transition jam before Fire On The Mountain is just four minutes and there's not much to it, except for Brent's interesting fingerings (7:14–).

Fire On The Mountain, verse one, Garcia mucks up some of the lyrics, but then lets loose with a few wild lines at the end of his first solo. He messes up the first line of the next verse, but once again unearths some interesting phrasing towards the end of the solo. Brent's ending lines evoke Springsteen piano sounds before they go to Drums.

The Other One starts underpowered. The first jam does have Brent's interesting tinkling sounds after the four-minute mark. Morning Dew feels unsteady, e.g., the "where have all the people gone" verse gets a bit screwed up at the end, both lyrics and chords (3:25–). The exit jam has an underwhelming build.

The Saturday Night encore sounds sluggish.

Link to recordings

1989 MOUNTAIN VIEW, CA

## SHORELINE AMPHITHEATRE

The middle concert here, there are just three songs post-Drums. Lots of MIDI guitar throughout the performance, from the Ramble On Rose solo to the final minutes of The Other One.

Set two, Scarlet Begonias, Garcia's fourth run on his inside solo busts out in phrases, perhaps assisted by the big push from Bill and Mickey.

The heart-of-gold-band-jam starts around 5:30, Garcia puts on his MIDI-flute about the eight-minute mark, later changing to a low-register bassoon, then back to throaty flute. They don't jam it into Fire On The Mountain, a mild surprise, as these days Fire is only a part-time dance partner. Women Are Smarter gets the floor.

Space is bells, flute, dungeon bassoon, ghostly medieval voices. On The Other One, Weir's first-verse vocals are choppily synthesized. The final minute turns avant-garde before yielding to Wharf Rat.

Deadbase X respondents gave nine other October 1989 performances votes, this got none (10/9/89 and 10/16/89 were rated first and second best for the year).

Link to recordings

### 1994 BOSTON, MA
## BOSTON GARDEN

Fourth night of six here, one of their best performances this year, especially set one, a great night for Garcia.

They begin with a crisp Help On The Way opener. Garcia's solo in Slipknot! evokes synthed-up shades of Terrapin Flyer (2:10–). What got into these guys? This kind of thing was not supposed to happen in 1994.

Franklin's Tower is amazing. Garcia's voice and soloing are bright, upbeat, and lucid.

Walking Blues is well done, including a great piano break from Vince. Then we get a positively bouncy Althea; is this 1982? Garcia's vocal phrasing is a must listen.

Big River features Vince's piano. Tom Thumb Blues highlights Garcia's sliding solo.

So Many Roads is taken at a quick pace and has a few minor vocal flubs. Then you will hear Garcia like never before. After 5:30, he's as strong and passionate as he ever was, in a brand-new way. Stunning.

The closing Promised Land actually, yes, rocks.

The energy carries over into set two. On Scarlet Begonias, Bill and Mickey come out bashing, and Vince creates a variation on the main theme. Towards the end of the jam, Garcia switches to MIDI-flute, Lesh starts his Fire On The Mountain bass line (11:33–), then Garcia mimics that line with his flute sound (11:44–).

The first Fire solo has speed! and flurried notes! (3:52–). There's sustained improvisation throughout the entire number and no vocal issues.

After the near half-hour couplet, they go straight into Way To Go Home, intent on continuing to rock the house. Saint Of Circumstance and Terrapin Station are next, rounding out an hour of music pre-Drums.

Even Stella Blue has some giddyap. Garcia noodles on it for over a minute before launching the vocal. There's a slight issue with line one, but otherwise it's well sung. The exit is four minutes long; turn it up to hear Lesh's counterpointing bass lines. Garcia plays around with some pretty melodic notes and a flowering motif (8:40–). In the final minute, he briefly reprises the Stella Blue sung refrain.

Deadbase respondents ranked this fifth best of the year, a vote ahead of 10/5/94. It should probably rank higher, e.g., ahead of 7/20/94. Headyversion voters ranked So Many Roads second best all-time (just behind 7/9/95).

Link to recordings

# OCTOBER 2

1966 San Francisco, CA, San Francisco State College, Commons

1968 San Mateo, CA, Pacific Recording
(studio) (no recording)

1969 Boston, MA, Boston Tea Party
(no setlist, no recording)

1972 Springfield, MA, Springfield Civic Center

1976 Cincinnati, OH, Riverfront Coliseum

1977 Portland, OR, Paramount Theater

1980 San Francisco, CA, Warfield Theater

1981 London, England, Rainbow Theater

1987 Mountain View, CA, Shoreline Amphitheatre

1988 Mountain View, CA, Shoreline Amphitheatre

1994 Boston, MA, Boston Garden

## 1966 SAN FRANCISCO, CA

# SAN FRANCISCO STATE COLLEGE, COMMONS

Apparently, there were no songs from the band's repertoire played at this iteration of the Trips Festival (Acid Test). The recordings mostly contain raps, interviews, and assorted sounds. Compare 1/8/66 and 3/12/66.

Link to recordings

## 1972 SPRINGFIELD, MA

# SPRINGFIELD CIVIC CENTER

A compelling sequence in set two begins with Truckin' and flows through Nobody's Fault But Mine and "Feelin' Groovy" jams before landing in Morning Dew.

Set one features a fifteen-minute Bird Song in the fifth spot, and a twenty-minute Playing In The Band before closing with Casey Jones.

In set two, after Truckin', we hear their third Nobody's Fault Jam (the most recent rendition appears on 6/13/70). The eight-minute Jam out of Drums is plenty jazzy at the start, Keith is prominent. Then Lesh alters his bass line and they evoke the "Feelin' Groovy" jam from '73–'74 China Cat → Rider transitions, a musical idea in embryo (Deadbase identifies this as the fourth and last "Uncle John's Jam") (see also 11/17/71, 11/8/69, and 9/27/69).

Double encore: Uncle John's Band and Johnny B. Goode.

Link to recordings

## 1976 CINCINNATI, OH

# RIVERFRONT COLISEUM

"If you folks don't quit throwin' things at us, we're gonna start throwin' 'em back." –BW

Amidst the flying flotsam and jetsam, another strong night on the Fall '76 Tour. Set two features an Other One sandwich with a Stella Blue filling.

The second frame starts with Music Never Stopped. After the inside jam, Garcia makes the usual turn to drive it home (3:43), but this time he goes somewhere else. Instead of the hard-rocking three chords, he solos over four chords that sound a bit like the Mind Left Body Jam (or perhaps it's the "keep on dancin' through to daylight" bridge). A minute later he returns to the normal rocked-out finish.

The concert's final sequence starts with Dancin' In The Streets, winds through Drums and comes out into The Other One.

Around 2:50 in The Other One, there are great licks from Garcia reminiscent of the old-style Irish jig he did in '68; then we get the Spanish Lady verse. It's all jamming after that until they wind it down and begin Stella Blue.

We hear a sublime exit solo, quivering and quaking with feeling, then the traditional ending. Garcia begins to stutter around a single note, and the drums kick it around. What's next?

They tiptoe back into The Other One and the lily fields verse, then Sugar Magnolia to close.

Link to recordings

## 1977 PORTLAND, OR
# PARAMOUNT THEATER

Second of two here, notable for the Casey Jones opener—their first version since October 1974, and it's over ten minutes long—as well as their first Dupree's Diamond Blues since 1969.

Casey Jones gains some length from a vocal glitch after the instrumental break. Garcia can't get the "trouble with you" verse started, so they go 'round the bend again. And again. And again! It amounts to eight runs down the track (3:49–6:50); Keith takes the last two.

El Paso has high-speed Garcia licks, and he's so amped up he nearly drowns Weir out during the "bullet goes deep in my chest" lyric (listen for Keith's Kentucky Derby "Call to the Post" ending) (4:11). A strong Let It Grow ends set one.

Set two, Fire On The Mountain (#16) is their first in four months. It has a long intro with the first verse coming around 2:35. Harpsichord sounds are sprinkled throughout. The back end of Garcia's first solo features a couple of 78-speed flurries (5:13, 5:23).

There's no "almost ablaze" middle verse. After the final "long distance runner" verse, we get the majestic descending scale to start the final break. It quiets around 10:39 until they sound the Scarlet Begonias exit theme at 11:30.

On the Sugar Magnolia closer, Bill and Mickey send the main jam into high gear, waves of rolls and still bashing hard on Sunshine Daydream.

A good performance, Deadbase respondents say ninth best this year (ranked higher than 5/5/77, 5/15/77, 11/2/77, and 11/5/77).

(Headyversion voters rank the Casey Jones best ever, by a wide margin).

Link to recordings

### 1980 SAN FRANCISCO, CA
## WARFIELD THEATER

Sixth night of the stand, their first ever acoustic Iko Iko (see also 10/7/80 and 10/26/80) and two Drums → Space segments.

Set three starts with Drums, four minutes worth, then a couple more minutes of Space; the latter mostly consists of Garcia's wanderings, hand drums, and bells. Out of this we hear Comes A Time. It is well done, one of only seven performed in 1980. The final two-chord outro jam sounds a lot like Lost Sailor and voila! they nicely segue into that one.

Terrapin Station into Playing In The Band precedes the other Drums → Space intermezzo. Stella Blue → Sugar Magnolia closes.

After twenty-seven songs, they still had the spunk for an Alabama Getaway encore.

Link to recordings

### 1981 LONDON, ENGLAND
## RAINBOW THEATER

The second night of the European tour, the first of three here.

In set two, the pre-Drums section is Playing In The Band → Shakedown Street → Bertha, then back to a Playin' jam. The set also includes a

Spanish Jam out of Space. You'll note plenty of hijinks in Weir's vocals throughout the evening, as well as considerable electric piano from Brent.

The opening Playing In The Band has a jam that starts low-key, later revealing some fast Egyptian runs from Garcia paired with Brent's electric piano sounding like an early '70s jam. Bill and Mickey start bashing in the final minute, Garcia whips out a few, slashing Shakedown Street chords then puts the hammer down, an interesting transition.

On Shakedown Street, Brent continues with the Chick Corea electric piano sound; there are some beautiful tones coming out of his rig. At the end of the jam, a surprising launch of an up-tempo Bertha.

Garcia takes an extra solo after the four-minute mark before the "ran into a rainstorm" verse. It leads to another singing of the chorus, and then…another solo! A peculiar rendition, as at the finish they go right back into a Playin'-style jam, with bunches of Garcia's speed licks and some fast Dark Starry fingerings at the end (3:45–).

The end of Space and Spanish Jam have more of Brent's electric piano, Bill and Mickey's military march, and Garcia drilling for oil on a single note (6:50; 8:14). A natural transition into Truckin' is halted by Weir's police whistle; he continues to ad-lib animated lyrics that began at the concert's set one opening with Minglewood Blues ("ever since, she went and had her sex changed…just ain't the same").

On Sugar Magnolia, Brent takes a fabulous organ solo to finish the main break as Garcia steps back (3:55–).

"Sunshine Daydream…come out and play!"

Encore: A spirited U.S. Blues.

Link to recordings

1987 MOUNTAIN VIEW, CA

## SHORELINE AMPHITHEATRE

First of three here, a week after the end of the East Coast tour. This is the first of thirty-nine concerts played at this venue.

Set one closes with Let It Grow, it's thirteen minutes long and well done. During the "rise and fall" jam, it sounds like they will pivot to the bridge (6:45–), but Garcia seems to want to plow ahead. They get there after eight minutes and stretch it out with interesting sounds layered from Brent and Weir.

The set two opening China Cat Sunflower rises to a nice peak, and the following I Know You Rider has some solid soloing. Women Are Smarter is its usual energetic self.

Post-Drums, after The Wheel, there's a bit of a mix-up on Gimme Some Lovin'. Lesh starts singing the first verse while Brent and the band keep playing the intro. After a few more bars, Lesh signals "hey!" and they get it just exactly perfect. The following lead vocals sound strong, with Lesh and Brent singing together.

On All Along The Watchtower (#15), Weir ends the first verse snarling, then he's near falsetto at the start of the second, a lively vocal performance. Garcia hits the note on his final solo (5:05), an exciting peak. They wind it down, then wind it back up with Garcia's long coda and a crashing halt. It's a natural concert closer, but for some reason they end with Don't Ease Me In.

Link to recordings

## 1988 MOUNTAIN VIEW, CA
# SHORELINE AMPHITHEATRE

The last of three here, they open set two with Crazy Fingers and place Space third in the order, well before Drums.

Bill and Mickey lead the transition out of Crazy Fingers smoothly, but it takes the rest of the band some time to hop aboard Samson & Delilah. After Samson, they do indeed play a Space section, Garcia and the drummers kind of propelling it into a near jam of sorts.

After Garcia engages his Mu-Tron, we hear a unique prelude to Estimated Prophet. Weir's closing Estimated vocals are raspy, urgent and half-crazed; then there's a short jam before Eyes Of The World.

At the end of Drums, we get another unique interlude, with Lesh playing a few bass notes on his own. It sounds more like tuning than a solo and certainly not anything resembling his solos from the '70s. It fades into more Space as he's overtaken by ocean liner sounds.

Link to recordings

## 1994 BOSTON, MA
# BOSTON GARDEN

Seven songs pre-Drums, including two of the new ones (Samba In The Rain, and If The Shoe Fits).

Garcia is in relatively decent voice, handling Loser and Row Jimmy well early in set one, along with quick hands on his guitar solo during Loser. Vince reels off some bright honky-tonk piano on It's All Over Now.

Set two, Crazy Fingers, Garcia's vocals are a bit iffy, but there's a plucky little solo, along with Weir's flanging, distorted squawking behind the singing. The exit jam is still a southern Mediterranean beauty.

The back half of That Would Be Something is a sluggish jam, thankfully ended by a Drums that starts with salsa. Then it's quiet hand percussion until five minutes in when we get synthed horn sounds. From there, it starts to get interesting, not quite Radiohead but New Age that's worthy of Tangerine Dream.

Garcia's Corrina-drone tone comes at the start of Space; he plays it for single notes followed by some very pretty sounds (3:25–) worthy of their own song and heralding some trumpet.

Space is not odd or jarring, it's more like something you might hear in the background at an acupuncture clinic, a perfect cerulean blue mood for entering Days Between. There's a vocal muff or two, but a grand soundscape, the main solo break, begins around 8:27.

Link to recordings

# OCTOBER 3

1968 San Mateo, CA, Pacific Recording
   (studio) (no recording)

1969 Boston, MA, Boston Tea Party
   (no setlist, no recording)

1976 Detroit, MI, Cobo Arena

1980 San Francisco, CA, Warfield Theater

1981 London, England, Rainbow Theater

1987 Mountain View, CA, Shoreline Amphitheatre

1994 Boston, MA, Boston Garden

1976 DETROIT, MI

## COBO ARENA

This is their third state in three days (Indiana, Ohio, Michigan) and the final concert outside California this year. There are super segues in set two. The journey begins with Playing In The Band and includes a Dancin' In The Streets → Not Fade Away sandwich near the end.

Playin' is the third song in set two, a fabulous fourteen-minute version featuring wonderful sustained improvisation that turns neither dark nor dissonant. In the final minute, a short Drums with hints of Dancin' In The Streets yields to a steady, Native American drumbeat paving the way to The Wheel.

That one finishes with a pretty exit jam. Keith is off to the races at the end of it, Garcia follows, and a new jam begins. It's generally percussive, Egyptian-style, until they slowly noodle before latching on to the Good Lovin' theme and launch that song. It's Weir's second try on this tune as lead vocalist (see also 10/20/74).

As they play the final chords of Good Lovin', Garcia steers a solo into new places. It has a brief happy feel at the start, soon pivoting into a darker, minor key. Around 1:45, you can hear Keith begin to play chords that resemble "Take Five," and Garcia picks up on it a couple of times. But they soon close it off to go elsewhere and find Comes A Time.

The exit jam there takes a turn around 8:30, with Garcia heading to points unknown and Keith vamping, no hint of what's next. Bill and Mickey pick out the beat for Dancin' In The Streets and off they go. The Dancin' jam has some great stuff from Keith after six minutes, a prime example of his jazz chops.

There's not much jamming in the intro to Not Fade Away; it takes them almost four minutes to get to the first verse. Not to worry: the middle of the jam is more interesting, including Weir picking out his China Cat lick (10:15–10:50).

They devolve into drumming by 11:45 before Garcia picks up the Not Fade Away theme again, only to let it go. They wander off once more until suddenly Lesh decides to take the lead, pumping out a bass line. Garcia scampers and abracadabra! the next line out of Lesh is his Dancin' In The Streets lead. They finish that song with a return to the bridge and the vocals.

It all gets a cherry on top with a Chuck Berry finish, Around And Around.

Link to recordings

## 1980 SAN FRANCISCO, CA
## WARFIELD THEATER

The third set features a Playing In The Band sandwich with Drums, Space, and The Wheel inside.

They end set two with Music Never Stopped. Garcia's racing, mercurial fills and passionate soloing are highlights on the inside and exit jams.

At the start of set three, that energy runneth over into the opening Scarlet Begonias, with Garcia displaying strong melodic command on the inside solo, three runs. Towards the end of the transition jam, after a couple of sky-high bends, he breaks out into two phrases with a bit of a Latin lilt (7:15–), then goes off on a mad, warbling dash for the door.

Lesh is there waiting with his Fire On The Mountain sledgehammer. It's always a treat to hear all three Fire verses sung strong and true.

One of the better electric sets of the Warfield stand, only Brokedown Palace made the *Dead Set* release.

Link to recordings

## 1981 LONDON, ENGLAND
# RAINBOW THEATER

Second of four here, a big night for straight ahead rock 'n' roll, they open with Alabama Getaway → Promised Land and close with Around And Around → One More Saturday Night. Also tonight: Morning Dew, one of seven this year.

The set one highlight is the eleven-minute Bird Song, Garcia racing like a thoroughbred alongside Brent's electric piano. It starts to slow down after six minutes but still percolates, a low boil of drums, piano, and guitar.

Feel Like A Stranger opens set two, and the jam starts to cook around 6:30. A minute later, some wonderfully strange synth tones come out of Brent's rig, then it's back to the main theme to finish it off.

On Not Fade Away, near the end of the main jam, Weir reprises the vocal chorus alone atop a darker motif that Lesh and Brent set in motion (8:30–). Morning Dew begins with some thick, church-like tones from Brent. They take it down as quiet as the vacuum of space (7:45) from which Brent's cathedral organ rises.

Encore: Brokedown Palace (more church).

Link to recordings

## 1987 MOUNTAIN VIEW, CA
## SHORELINE AMPHITHEATRE

A great night for Brent, he shines everywhere, and his broad palette of sounds are on full display.

Hey Pocky Way (#5) opens, he gets the first solo and carries the tune. Listen to him tear the roof off the final phrase of the last sung verse: "rock 'n' roll."

Set two starts with Maggie's Farm (#5) → Cumberland Blues. As they tune up, Brent tries his violin effect (used in When I Paint My Master-piece in set one but not here). Garcia starts it off with the same riff he uses on Big River. From there, they move into Cumberland without a hitch. Brent's playing on both of these sparkles.

On Looks Like Rain, Weir's finale is a long one (4:30–), and Brent steals the show with his Hornsby-like piano lines. After Weir's "listen!" (7:30) Brent's notes are soon drowned out by Garcia who adds a unique coda. Terrapin Station features a rousing finish.

Post-Space, Brent's fills on The Other One are delightfully discordant, and the band packs a high-energy jam into a shortish, two-verse version. Stella Blue gets Brent's harpsichord-like accompaniment. The start of Garcia's inside solo is on overdrive, as big as all outdoors.

Garcia finishes the song by picking out the first few notes of Turn On Your Lovelight, but they do Throwing Stones first.

Encore: Mighty Quinn.

Deadbase respondents rank this seventh best of the year (Headyversion voters rate Candyman as eighth best all-time).

Link to recordings

1994 BOSTON, MA
## BOSTON GARDEN

Some old chestnuts are sprinkled here and there (three from *American Beauty*) along with an unusual pre-Drums pairing of Cassidy → Goin' Down The Road Feelin' Bad.

There's a great surprise in the second spot, Beat It On Down The Line; only a handful were performed each year in this era (this one turned out to be their last; it was played every year except for 1976). Loose Lucy has surprisingly strong singing from Garcia (dig the final chorus!).

Bird Song begins with over-amplified avian sounds, it's a thirteen-minute version that closes set one. Five minutes in, they head outside the lines for some dissonant jazz. Vince creates a dashing piano run (7:25–) and then another (8:30–); the fever breaks around the ten-minute mark.

Set two, after a Box Of Rain opener, we get nearly seventeen minutes of Shakedown Street. There's some snap, crackle, and pop to this version of the Disco Era weave, though some of the occasional synth licks from Vince are cringeworthy (but watch him shine at the end of the first solo break, a beautiful piano run, 4:17–4:31).

On Cassidy, Weir's guitar seems to be on distorted, flanging autopilot, but there's sterling guitar work from Garcia during the jam, bright and articulate. They seem intent on ending it around the six-minute mark, but it turns out to be a mirage (did they intend to keep going or just miss the stop sign?).

Encore: Brokedown Palace, appropriate for what turned out to be the last of their twenty-four appearances here (Boston Garden closed for good on 9/28/95; the band was scheduled to close the venue with shows on 9/13/95 through 9/19/95).

This performance is among the Deadbase respondents top twenty for the year, worth a full listen for the '94-inclined or those simply curious.

Link to recordings

# OCTOBER 4

1968 San Mateo, CA, Pacific Recording
(studio) (no recording)

1969 Boston, MA, Boston Tea Party
(no setlist, no recording)

1970 San Francisco, CA, Winterland Ballroom

1980 San Francisco, CA, Warfield Theater

1981 London, England, Rainbow Theater

1987 Mountain View, CA, Shoreline Amphitheatre

## 1970 SAN FRANCISCO, CA

# WINTERLAND BALLROOM

We have ten songs plus a bit of Truckin', including the second of only five performances of Till The Morning Comes.

The recordings have the sixth earliest Brokedown Palace currently available. Lesh is up in the mix here and on China Cat Sunflower, his lines a shining example of why he belonged in the same sentence with his contemporaries, a golden era of jamming rock bassists (Jack Casady, Jack Bruce, John Paul Jones, Entwistle, Oakley, etc.). Garcia kind of quotes There Is A Mountain/Mountain Jam right before they go into I Know You Rider.

In Good Lovin', at 3:18 of the longer jam, the band trades fours, with the drummers, Lesh and Weir, each getting their turn. Out of this, they come together on the main theme and ride it strong back into Pigpen.

Some great 1970 sound here.

Link to recordings

## 1980 SAN FRANCISCO, CA

# WARFIELD THEATER

Three sets, thirty-two songs. They play their first Deep Elem Blues in ten years. Deal has the new exit jam.

Set one is acoustic and features a great piano solo by Brent on The Race Is On. Garcia's solo on It Must Have Been The Roses is sublime. Specifically, during his improvisation in the third line of the verse (4:38–4:45), the notes he chooses are an astounding surprise, a great example of one of his countless musical leaps of faith. Monkey & The Engineer has another Brent piano solo, two runs. Great.

They flip a switch and go electric, launching into Alabama Getaway to start set two. But it doesn't sound strong, Garcia's playing is underwhelming, and the following Greatest Story is also kind of unsteady. Next is Candyman and they sound in sync, more comfortable than on the up-tempo numbers. The set closes with Deal, the additional jam at the end in its fiery infancy (4:08–5:02).

Set three has a rocking close, I Need A Miracle → Johnny B. Goode. They neatly shift keys towards the end of Miracle to transition without a hitch. It's a spectacular finish by Garcia as he unleashes a tornado of chords (there is some of that action on the Not Fade Away chorus).

Double encore: Uncle John's Band into One More Saturday Night (one of two double encores on this stand) (see 10/14/80).

Not among the best Warfield concerts, but perhaps a quality SBD of the whole thing will prove differently (perhaps not).

Link to recordings

### 1981 LONDON, ENGLAND
## RAINBOW THEATER

Dynamite from the get-go. Weir is in rare form before the show starts, rapping about an equipment issue, then taking a poll about a movie (see 12/7/79 for another one of his polls).

But the real tip-off is Jack Straw, Garcia's fill inside the final sung chorus, a screaming, hair-raising lick after the "half a mile from Tucson" line (1/7/78 Jack Straw has similarly inspired fills). Wow.

Set two, six songs pre-Drums. Before they finish the opening Cold Rain & Snow, the drummers start up Samson & Delilah. As they all vamp, Weir explains their choice: "This bein' Sunday, we thought we'd do a...spiritual number."

Brent hammers the Hammond, channeling Jimmy Smith. Garcia goes supersonic (e.g., 3:12–3:25). Weir tears into the vocals.

"I would tear this ol' building down (wouldn't be hard)." –BW

Scarlet Begonias is next. Garcia takes six runs on his inside solo, hitting two beautiful high notes at the end of his fourth run, mostly chords after that. He starts a staccato festival (12:03–) before they head into Fire On The Mountain. His solo after the "almost ablaze" verse is a 78-speed whirling dervish (6:07–). There are more peaks at the end of the final jam.

Weir is up next with Lost Sailor. Mach speed, nonstop noodling from Garcia on the exit. On Saint Of Circumstance, the rain-fallin'-down jam features Hurricane Jerry. Plus Weir's vocal cherry on top: "Some folks dream their lives away, now; they may settle for a time in a Chevrolet, now."

Space, four minutes in, has some interesting solo lines. What's next? Garcia hints at The Other One, but first it's a Spanish Jam. An interesting transition into The Other One from there, they clear a path for Lesh and we quickly get verse one. Listen for the final transition back to the second verse. Smoking.

Weir: "Sunshine Daydream…just come on out and *play*!"

Lively to brilliant 1981, deserving of far more recognition.

Link to recordings

## 1987 MOUNTAIN VIEW, CA
# SHORELINE AMPHITHEATRE

Sunday, the last night of the tour, and their 75th performance of the year. They pump it up a bit with an Iko Iko set one closer, and Devil With The Blue Dress → Good Golly Miss Molly in set two. But it sounds more pleasant than rocking.

A strong Jack Straw opens, but the momentum slows with Push Comes To Shove. Weir climbing a singer's Everest—Bob Dylan's "Desolation Row"—is always a treat. Iko Iko is short, and so is this set (six songs, like 9/18/87, which offered La Bamba in the next frame).

Set two: Hell In A Bucket is an up-tempo prelude (intense echo on Weir's exit vocals) for Devil With The Blue Dress (#5 of five) and Good Golly Miss Molly (#3 of three). Then it's back to Weir for Estimated Prophet. He seems to have the most energy tonight, his vocals dancing.

Double encore: Touch Of Grey, Brokedown Palace.

Link to recordings

# OCTOBER 5

1968 Sacramento, CA, Memorial Auditorium
(no setlist, no recording)

1969 Houston, CA, Sam Houston Coliseum
(no setlist, no recording)

1970 San Francisco, CA, Winterland Ballroom
(partial setlist, no recording)

1984 Charlotte, NC, Charlotte Coliseum

1994 Philadelphia, PA, The Spectrum

1984 CHARLOTTE, NC
## CHARLOTTE COLISEUM

After a two-and-a-half-month break, they start the Fall tour on a Friday night here. After a somewhat promising opening—Bertha → Promised Land—it begins to go downhill. West L.A. Fadeaway is next (it's mostly sluggish) then Little Red Rooster, including an unremarkable slide solo from Garcia and the usual awful slide solo from Weir. Then it gets worse.

Brown Eyed Women has a uniquely strange start; either it's startlingly inventive improv (unlikely) or memory loss experienced by Garcia and the drummers. The sonically struggling vocals don't help.

On Feel Like A Stranger, they play the intro, and it seems like Weir misses his vocal cue, or perhaps he's just taking his time. Something is definitely not exactly perfect, because after the first verse (1:10ish) they play their instruments when in fact the next verse should be sung ("well the music's thunderin'"). Later, Garcia plays his lines signaling the end of the jam (9:54–), but the rest of the band doesn't even acknowledge (or remember?) it.

Set two is similarly troubled. They seem together during the China Cat jam, Garcia signals the peak (7:19), and the rest of the band joins. But during I Know You Rider, he muffs the end of his "headlight" verse (singing "my mind was wanderin'" instead of "I'd shine my light"). At least his fingers still know the way.

Spacey sounds emerge from somewhere during the height of Garcia's inside solo on Estimated Prophet (4:45–). He goes into frenzied noodling (11:00–) that Brent briefly mimics (11:39) as they transition into Eyes Of The World. This goes well; there's more assured singing from

Garcia, a crisp pace, and some interesting riffing from Brent in the final minutes.

Space is compelling. They tease a Spanish Jam after the seven-minute mark and keep it up for about a minute. The Other One is one of the better numbers of the night, they do both verses. On Black Peter, Garcia sings the "fever rolled up" verse (2:35–), solos, and then sings the same verse again (4:55–).

They have some trouble starting Sugar Magnolia. It's another one where nobody seems to remember how it goes. A minute in, Bill and Mickey wipe the slate clean with drum rolls so they can try again. The main jam ends around 7:30, and instead of going into Sunshine Daydream, we get Johnny B. Goode, with a fine, ringing solo by Brent.

No customary "thank you" from Weir.

Encore: Baby Blue.

Link to recordings

## 1994 PHILADELPHIA, PA
## THE SPECTRUM

The first of three here, they continue a fine run that began in Boston, Garcia singing and picking well. Set two has a rare In The Midnight Hour opener, a seventeen-minute Uncle John's Band, and Garcia joining Drums.

Set one, Wang Dang Doodle, Vince's organ solo is quite good. He takes an interesting piano solo on Queen Jane, briefly quoting from a famous piece of classical music (4:10–). And on the closing Deal, he gets a big

solo on the exit (6:20–) and finishes with a flourish, the crowd respond-
ing in kind. A long exit jam, Garcia takes it to different places with a bit
of a Dark Starish jig starting around ten minutes in.

Set two, Midnight Hour, the lead vocals are a Weir-Vince duo. We also
hear some synth horn fills, and what sounds like a mushy MIDI Garcia
solo. Cumberland Blues has a flash of the old bluegrassy speed (6:30).

The main meal starts with Playing In The Band. It becomes moderately
dissonant during the jam, then Garcia starts something new after nine
minutes before a sweet transition into Uncle John's Band, with Vince
briefly quoting again from a classical piece (this one is Bach's "Jesu, Joy
of Man's Desiring").

The exit jam goes full avant-garde after thirteen minutes and then
intensely wiggy like the spacey part of a '70s Other One jam. The fever
breaks (14:45), then builds again.

Drums starts with as many sounds as skins. Garcia joins with distorted
guitar around 4:45. Halfway through Space, we hear some Victim Or
The Crime tones.

For Standing On The Moon, Garcia is in fine voice, and you can hear it
early, e.g., "I *watch* it all roll by." His voice is also strong on the encore,
Mighty Quinn, with no strain and no cracks.

Deadbase respondents have this as sixth best of the year, a single vote
behind 10/1/94 (Headyversion voters rank Standing On The Moon
seventh best all-time).

Link to recordings

# OCTOBER 6

1966 San Francisco, CA, Golden Gate Park, The Panhandle
(no setlist, no recording)

1969 San Francisco, CA, Family Dog at The Great Highway
(no setlist, no recording)

1977 Tempe, AZ, Arizona State University, ASU Activity Center

1980 San Francisco, CA, Warfield Theater

1981 London, England, Rainbow Theater

1984 Richmond, VA, Richmond Coliseum

1994 Philadelphia, PA, The Spectrum

1977 TEMPE, AZ

## ARIZONA STATE UNIVERSITY, ASU ACTIVITY CENTER

The seven recordings we have are problematic; it's unclear which songs are actually from this date. Some of this concert was broadcast on the FM King Biscuit Hour.

Not Fade Away is the must listen, what a pace! Garcia doesn't hit the brakes for six minutes and is soon off to the races again. But how much of the Drums and the Not Fade Away before Black Peter is from this date?

Around And Around is blistering, another lucid Chuck Berry master class (check out Garcia's spooky, awesome bends around the 5:00 mark). Maybe the Dead's archivist will make sense of the archaeology.

Link to recordings

1980 SAN FRANCISCO, CA

## WARFIELD THEATER

After a day of rest on Sunday, the band performs its ninth of fifteen on this stand. Garcia is on his game.

The first electric set opens with China Cat Sunflower → I Know You Rider and we get crisp soloing, especially on Rider, with a fabulous rave-up on the final run. Lazy Lightnin' → Supplication is played for the second time on this stand. It's a lot of energy for the middle of a set with stunning soloing towards the end.

In the final set, It Must Have Been The Roses is performed electric for one of only two times during the Warfield/Radio City series (see

10/2/80). Post-Space, the transition into The Other One starts in the final minute of Truckin'. Between the Spanish lady and lily fields verses, the jam builds to a wild peak, not to be missed.

They close with a Sugar Magnolia that bypasses Sunshine Daydream and goes straight into Johnny B. Goode (see also 10/5/84).

Link to recordings

## 1981 LONDON, ENGLAND
# RAINBOW THEATER

The final night of four here, the He's Gone and Blues for Allah tease in Space are likely nods to Anwar Sadat, President of Egypt, assassinated earlier that day. There's an additional set two surprise: the Sunshine Daydream portion of Sugar Magnolia is served up as one of two encores.

Set one is heavy with love-gone-wrong songs (Althea, Looks Like Rain) and blues (Minglewood, Mexicali, Cumberland). Brent adds to these tales of woe with his new blues, Never Trust A Woman aka Good Times (#6).

There's some fine lead guitar playing in the first set. It Must Have Been The Roses in the third spot features a beautifully expressive solo, especially over the first two lines of the verse. On Althea, after the "space is getting hot" lyric, Garcia reels off a fantastic run up the hill. His final solo has many flourishes.

Set two starts with their newish cover, Man Smart, Woman Smarter (#8), Weir in full bloom. Garcia vaguely quotes from Blues for Allah about four minutes into Space, and again around 6:30. The Wheel starts with some pedal-steel-like sounds from Brent. They take their time playing around with the lovely theme for over three minutes.

Sugar Magnolia usually signals the close, but here they pass the baton to two more tunes, starting with Stella Blue. The start of the exit jam is exquisite, but the end proves to be a challenging transition from the motif Garcia is chomping on into Good Lovin'.

"I wished I had somebody to help me say it now…I wanna tell ya about a friend of mine…a one and only kind…" –BW

Encore: Sunshine Daydream, then Brokedown Palace.

Link to recordings

## 1984 RICHMOND, VA
# RICHMOND COLISEUM

They seem to find their footing here. Set one is all old-school, mid '70s or earlier but for the Hell In A Bucket opener.

In set one, Garcia pushes the envelope on some of his solos. On They Love Each Other, there are two main runs (4:02–, 5:12–); the second is a nonstop, mad dash. Tennessee Jed, the end of the solo, he pushes higher and higher until shattering the ceiling. Weir infuses Looks Like Rain with the power of a set-closing anthem, but they tack on Don't Ease Me In before hitting the dressing room.

Set two also leans to the '70s for the song list, except for the post-Space → Throwing Stones. Scarlet Begonias opens on all cylinders, and the transition jam begins with some Caribbean percussion. The last verse of Fire On The Mountain has a slight stumble early, but Garcia delivers the goods on the final line.

Playing In The Band is next, there's a pretty start to the jam; Lesh and Garcia's lines intertwine, an interesting version. Where will it go?

There's no doubt after Brent brushes the canvas with harpsichord, as Garcia quickly follows with the first verse of China Doll. At the end of the exit jam, Brent takes the melody and delivers a Garcia-like run (6:34–). Then they start something brand-new, exploring for five minutes before yielding to Drums.

Bill and Mickey get off to a fast start, and the following Space has feedbacking amps and ghostly sheets of sound. When Brent joins a few minutes in, he turns it into a Jam, mostly a trio with Weir and Lesh. Garcia is in for the last two minutes.

They play a strange, sluggish Throwing Stones until Weir comes alive in the final minute. Garcia fingers the Goin' Down The Road intro lick as Weir is still singing the "ashes, ashes" refrain. One More Saturday Night closes.

A decent performance. You may wish for a soundboard recording.

Link to recordings

## 1994 PHILADELPHIA, PA
## THE SPECTRUM

An up-tempo Mississippi Half Step starts the night, one of the better late-era versions. The rest of the first set is less compelling, with an Easy Answers → Don't Ease Me In close.

Set two: not a single ballad before Drums. China Cat Sunflower opens, Vince playing Weir's classic circuitous lick. A perky rendition, it chugs along for eight minutes until I Know You Rider.

After Way To Go Home, the setlist goes retro, all 1971 or earlier. There's not much of a build in Truckin', it falls apart on the way up. Around the ten-minute mark, Bill and Mickey take over.

At the end of Space, Garcia starts The Other One theme with his MIDI flute.

Link to recordings

# OCTOBER 7

1966 San Francisco, CA, Winterland Ballroom
(or Fillmore Auditorium)

1968 San Mateo, CA, Pacific Recording
(studio) (no recording)

1977 Albuquerque, NM, University of New Mexico,
University Arena

1980 San Francisco, CA, Warfield Theater

1994 Philadelphia, PA, The Spectrum

## 1966 SAN FRANCISCO, CA

# WINTERLAND BALLROOM

We have just three songs: Cream Puff War, Good Morning Little School-girl, and Stealin'. But they appear to be from another date, and Deadbase indicates the concert was actually at the Fillmore Auditorium.

Link to recordings

## 1977 ALBUQUERQUE, NM

# UNIVERSITY OF NEW MEXICO,
# UNIVERSITY ARENA

The band heads 409 miles east and 4,000 feet higher to perform this Friday night gig. Set one seems to be unavailable, set two features both paradise lost and found.

Terrapin Station has some major vocal miscues; it becomes a musical misadventure lasting nearly fifteen minutes. Garcia skips the third verse ("shadows of a sailor"), then whiffs on the verse after the lion's den ("which of you to gain me, tell"). After the band goes around twice, Garcia leapfrogs all the way back to sing the "shadows" verse.

After singing that one, and the next, he gets lost again. Keith briefly solos, then Garcia starts his own (4:16–). That solo ends, but no verse follows, so Keith solos again. Garcia finally gets to the next two verses, then solos. The rest of the song goes better; the exit jam is just three minutes.

Sugar Magnolia is the clear star of the show. Bill and Mickey set a great tempo putting the band in the pocket. Garcia in '77 often captured the melodic heart of this song in his solos, and this is one of those. He switches over to chords after five minutes, then comes out swinging, brandishing brilliant bends before going completely bonkers. Marvelous.

Other high points of the set include a subdued, introspective jam in Playing In The Band, and Wharf Rat, with its beautiful gospel bridge and Garcia's fast, ascending repeating runs at the end of the exit jam.

Link to recordings

## 1980 SAN FRANCISCO, CA
# WARFIELD THEATER

Another marvel on Market Street. Set one features their first acoustic El Paso since 1970, and another acoustic Iko Iko; this one opens the set.

In the first electric set, Weir is in his usual strong voice on Let It Grow. Listen for Lesh's bass notes percolating underneath. On the closing Deal, there's an inside solo bright and brash, two runs, plus the new, rousing exit jam.

After a break, we get another electric set, this one opens with Shakedown Street. The transition from Estimated Prophet to He's Gone is swift; the first verse comes quickly. Post-Space, The Wheel's exit jam turns mysterious around five minutes. It has the cadence of a Playin' jam, with no hint of where they may be going.

Stella Blue gets pindrop quiet during the final verse, Garcia's voice lowers to a lone whisper in a room of 2,300 souls. From there, a beautifully expressive exit solo with a mesmerizing peak.

I Need A Miracle starts with the rollicking cadence of Dylan's "Highway 61 Revisited." A great rocking exit jam, they ride it into Good Lovin'.

Encore: Plenty left in the tank for Alabama Getaway.

Link to recordings

## 1994 PHILADELPHIA, PA
### THE SPECTRUM

"God bless The Grateful Dead." The band's 50th performance at this venue. Perhaps not without a sense of irony, or humor, they open with Feel Like A Stranger.

The first set is mostly older material, five of seven from the '70s. There's some good jamming in Stranger, and Garcia is game for tackling another big one next, Sugaree. After nine minutes, he even pulls off his whirling dervish licks. The crowd seems to finish his final sentence: "just don't tell 'em you (know-oh me)."

Set two is generally the newer stuff (Samba In The Rain, Corrina), but for the Morning Dew closer. At the start of Foolish Heart, Vince's piano is up, a promising Chuck Leavell, Jessica-like opportunity if he wanted it. During Garcia's solo, there are some nice piano chords from Vince, for awhile.

Morning Dew closes the concert, their first rendition in three months (see 7/20/94). A lovely "it doesn't matter anyway" refrain from Garcia is filled with emotion. Wow.

Link to recordings

# OCTOBER 8

1966 Marin County, CA, Mt. Tamalpais Amphitheatre
(no setlist, no recording)

1966 San Francisco, CA, Fillmore Auditorium
(no setlist, no recording)

1968 San Francisco, CA, The Matrix, San Francisco
(Mickey and the Heartbeats)

1981 Copenhagen, Denmark, Forum Theater

1983 Richmond, VA, Richmond Coliseum

1984 Worcester, MA, The Centrum

1989 Hampton, VA, Hampton Coliseum

## 1968 SAN FRANCISCO, CA
## THE MATRIX

No Weir or Pigpen, so this 1968 October run was billed as "Mickey and the Heartbeats." Cosmic Charlie, apparently the first one, is well recorded and fun. We also have the first recorded version of The Seven (the full band's first version appears to be on 9/29/69).

The twelve-minute Dark Star Jam (#3) has no verses; you'll mostly hear Garcia, Lesh, and the shaking percussion instrument. After the two-minute mark, Garcia plays only chords for awhile.

Many unnamed jams comprise the bulk of the sixteen tracks. A few have Jack Casady on bass (tracks eight through eleven). Elvin Bishop and the remnants of his band take over at track twelve.

Link to recordings

## 1981 COPENHAGEN, DENMARK
## FORUM THEATER

One night only here, very long versions of Scarlet → Fire (thirty minutes) and the Playin' → Terrapin couplet (twenty-seven minutes), but they are not having their best night. Many vocal hiccups.

There is strong soloing on Cumberland Blues, but Weir starts singing too early, then jumps the gun again before Garcia's first solo is finished. Later, Weir sounds nearly off-key, and forgets to start singing after Garcia plays the bridge. A real mess, and he knows it: "We gotta fix somethin.'" –BW

Cassidy is next, no problems there. Loser has more fine soloing, two runs. Althea is a bit sluggish, though on the final break Garcia picks out the melody and then explodes with a stutter step (7:21–). Brent's solos on They Love Each Other and C.C. Rider are great.

During The Music Never Stopped, the middle jam sounds odd; perhaps it's the mix, as if Brent's licks are in a different key than Garcia's. But there's a head-splitting, stuttering blast from the lead guitar around the eight-minute mark.

Set two, they seem to be in better shape. During the Scarlet jam we can finally hear some bass notes from Lesh, and Garcia's singing on Fire On The Mountain is robust.

On Playing In The Band, Weir attacks the lyrics with force but seems on the verge of more vocal accidents. Garcia's fast soloing stands out, Egyptian-flavored noodles.

Terrapin Station is fine, with Lesh up in the mix during the last few minutes. As it seems to end, around 13:30, they launch into a new jam. Will they go back to Playing In The Band? Or go somewhere new? They hand it over to Bill and Mickey.

A strange Space leads to a strange start to Not Fade Away, but it's a good strange. In the final minute, there's some inventive lead guitar phrases. They leave Denmark rocking out on more classics (Chuck Berry) and a wave of the flag (U.S. Blues encore).

Link to recordings

1983 RICHMOND, VA

# RICHMOND COLISEUM

This is the first night of the Fall East Coast tour, and their first visit to this city in over six years. A rare Crazy Fingers and an aborted Sugar Magnolia appear in set two. Generally, they sound ready rather than rusty, perhaps benefitting from the prior month's performances.

There's considerable energy in set one, from the Feel Like A Stranger opener, with Garcia's heavy Mu-Tron sound, to the Hell In A Bucket and Deal closer, with its raging exit jam. There are a few vocal mumbles from the lead guitarist, but his strings sparkle. On Brown Eyed Women, he takes three solo runs, gushing like mountain whitewater.

Most won't like the set two opener (Day Job), but stick around for Playing In The Band into Crazy Fingers. A great Playin' jam, after the ten-minute mark Weir sort of sounds out the four-note James Bond theme several times. On Crazy Fingers, Garcia's voice is strained but he solos sweetly on the exit; it's their first rendition of this song in a year, and the only one for the next two years.

And that's it, just those three songs before Drums. After Wharf Rat, Garcia and the drummers play Sugar Magnolia for a full minute, but Weir doesn't sing it, so at 1:07 of this "jam" they head into Good Lovin'.

Surprisingly good '83, worth a full listen despite receiving no votes from Deadbase X respondents (other October dates, starting with 10/11/83, get their nod).

Link to recordings

## 1984 WORCESTER, MA
# THE CENTRUM

Terrapin Station opens set two and leads to a unique pre-Drums section, including a cover of Willie Dixon's I Just Want To Make Love To You, just their third version since 1966 (see also 7/22/84). They won't try it again until 2/21/95.

Iko Iko opens the concert—it became a regular starter this year—with some fine phrases leaping out of Garcia's guitar. Weir's work on Bird Song and Supplication is interesting. Deal closes, a rousing exit jam, capping a strong first set.

Set two: Terrapin has a longish exit jam, but it seems to be running out of steam a couple of minutes in; it's not one of the symphonic festivals they often render. Then something wonderful happens: a brand-new jam is born, and the final two minutes they wander into the who knows where. Alas, Garcia pulls the plug on it, as you hear him raise his signature Samson & Delilah lick.

The Willie Dixon tune quickly follows; it's taken at a fast Cumberland Blues-like tempo. With Brent singing lead, it rolls on for nine minutes. Garcia gets into some high-speed licks, perhaps a bit like a Samson jam.

They turn on a dime and neatly segue into I Need A Miracle. It's a long version (thirteen minutes), but the second half of the jam really plods along, then wanders; this is not a 1978 barnburner. After the eleven-minute mark, it picks up and there are hints of The Other One, but it's more of a unique jam.

Link to recordings

1989 HAMPTON, VA

## HAMPTON COLISEUM

The first night of the East Coast tour, Garcia plays his Wolf guitar. The highlight is the set two opener, their first Help On The Way → Slipknot! in four years (9/12/85).

In the first set, Bird Song has a spacey halo through the jam before Garcia goes to his MIDI flute. After seven minutes, he begins the usual two-chord run. The closing Promised Land gets an added lift from Brent's ringing organ parts.

Set two, Help On The Way, oh those beautiful high bass notes. Garcia's MIDI is engaged on his Slipknot! solo, a near-bassoon sound, and there are other interesting tonescapes from Brent. The restatement of the theme before going into Franklin's Tower is a bit tentative.

In Eyes Of The World, around 7:45, the jam seems to end but they keep going for another minute or so. Morning Dew features an unusually raved-up inside solo, Garcia going to his blurred chording early, a treat.

Encore: We Bid You Goodnight (one of six this year), your early '70s dream come true.

Deadbase respondents rated this performance tied for third best this year with 10/26/89, but far behind the next night and 10/16/89 (Headyversion voters rated this version of Bird Song eleventh best all-time).

Link to recordings

# OCTOBER 9

1966 San Francisco, CA, Fillmore Auditorium
(no setlist, no recording)

1968 San Francisco, CA, The Matrix
(Mickey and the Heartbeats) (setlist, no recording)

1972 San Francisco, CA, Winterland Ballroom

1976 Oakland, CA, Oakland Coliseum

1977 Denver, CO, McNichols Sports Arena

1980 San Francisco, CA, Warfield Theater

1982 Palo Alto, CA, Stanford University, Frost Amphitheater

1983 Greensboro, NC, Greensboro Coliseum

1984 Worcester, MA, The Centrum

1989 Hampton, VA, Hampton Coliseum

1994 Landover, MD, USAir Arena

1972 SAN FRANCISCO, CA

## WINTERLAND BALLROOM

"Get that bitch off the stage." That's Grace Slick's prophetic parting shot after her short, screechy, set-two opening "Jam."

Otherwise, a fine performance. The set-one thrills include their second Box Of Rain ("that was Donna Jean" –PL) (see 9/17/70); the still up-tempo version of Friend Of The Devil; and the first set-ending Playing In The Band, twenty minutes worth.

The Playin' jam is full steam ahead until near the nine-minute mark; then the guitars catch their breath and Keith unreels some wonderful piano lines. They are soon stomping hard again, making it up as they go, reaching another great peak around the fifteen-minute mark (Weir is a real driver here). Garcia touches on the Playin' theme as they near twenty minutes, and then it's cut (ouch!), though it was likely near its natural end.

Set two: the He's Gone opener cleanses the stage of Grace Slick. An early Big River (#13) has plenty of hard country bite.

On Truckin', the jam starts to end after nine minutes and seems headed directly into The Other One after Bill changes up the rhythm, but we get a Lesh solo instead.

They navigate a smooth transition into The Other One. After the first verse, we hear some fat notes from Lesh and a general slowing of the tempo. A new jam starts around 4:25 and off they go, Weir the main instigator. Then Garcia leads a slick return to the Other One theme.

There's a great intro to the closing Sugar Magnolia: Weir's lead lick, Bill's crisp rolls and cymbal bashes, then Lesh rumbling up from the bottom.

1972 Grateful Dead; resistance is futile.

Link to recordings


## 1976 OAKLAND, CA

# OAKLAND COLISEUM

An outdoor gig, Bill Graham's Day On The Green #8, the band opens late morning for The Who.

A super set two, seamless top to bottom featuring a double sandwich: a St. Stephen opener jammed into and out of Not Fade Away, and a bifurcated Slipknot! with Drums and Samson & Delilah inside.

After the "one man gathers" line, they skip the usual St. Stephen inside jam and launch a nearly twelve-minute version of Not Fade Away. Not a particularly interesting jam, but a confident segue back into St. Stephen. So what's the answer to The Answer Man?

It's Help On The Way. Garcia is on his game, a fine version. Slipknot! gets quiet as a mouse three minutes in and Garcia turns on his underwatery guitar effect. They softly move into Drums, and then perfectly back out to Samson & Delilah. Tight.

At the end of Samson, Garcia restarts the Egyptian-style Slipknot! jam a single beat after a dead stop. There's some unique phrasing around 4:30, followed by shrieking bends before they start the song's rise.

In Franklin's Tower, solo number two starts all chords followed by frenetic frolicking, rising to an ecstatic peak around the five-minute mark. Then there's the quiet break, with pretty picking. Towards the end of the final break, Garcia pulls out his trilled chords. A great version.

Set one is also worth a visit, e.g., Scarlet Begonias; the jam has blizzards of notes and much more.

Deadbase respondents anointed this concert best of 1976, edging out 12/31/76 and 7/18/76.

Link to recordings

## 1977 DENVER, CO

# McNICHOLS SPORTS ARENA

The Sugaree and Music Never Stopped set one closer give an indication of the rising power of the band's performances this fall.

Start with Sugaree. The second break begins with Keith, then Garcia is off and running as they approach the seven-minute mark. He begins to nail some repeated patterns, then blasts into head-splitting trilled chords (7:57–). But it ain't over yet. Bill and Mickey join the fun, slashing and bashing, then Garcia returns to his high-speed drilling for aural oil or perhaps The Almighty. Powerful stuff.

The Music Never Stopped follows, with more manna from Garcia (seven runs of trilled chords at the end).

Set two starts with Samson & Delilah. As Reverend Gary Davis used to say, "Good God!" Clearly, this is a band out to kill. Bill and Mickey are again exuberant at the end.

On Estimated Prophet, the exit jam has the deep version of Garcia's Mu-Tron sound. There's a slick slowdown near the finish that ambles into He's Gone, a semi-regular dance partner at this time. Garcia goes for a bit of a solo stroll, forming part of a long intro (the first verse comes at 1:40).

Truckin' exhibits an exciting exit jam; they launch right into the build after the verses, Garcia driving them to the peak before they motor forward, swinging and stomping. Around And Around is the closer, a great version, with a well-orchestrated slow down and rebuild.

Quite good.

Link to recordings

## 1980 SAN FRANCISCO, CA
# WARFIELD THEATER

After a day off, the first of another round of three straight here. High-quality playing, even on the humblest of tunes.

Set two: they open with Feel Like A Stranger. After jamming for a while, Garcia sounds the theme (5:15–), but rather than signaling the end of the tune as in later years, they keep on jamming. He then goes on to create an interesting variation of the theme (6:35–).

Little Red Rooster starts spookily subdued. Brent's solo is tinkly piano rather than ringing organ, and Weir's slide solo steers clear of the highest parts of his fretboard.

On Tennessee Jed, the tempo is particularly plodding, counterbalanced by Garcia's boisterous singing. Music Never Stopped closes the set, the inside jam comes together nicely, Weir's jangling chords indicating the turn.

Set three: Alabama Getaway → Greatest Story opens, the Swiss watch at work. High Time appears for the second time on the Warfield stand (just once at Radio City). Delicate, the rhythm is held together by gossamer threads, Garcia's singing at times is no more than a whisper.

Lost Sailor is a prime example of their beautiful ensemble work. Garcia's solo (3:31–) starts with staccato lines, as Bill and Mickey place little drumbeats perfectly on his heels. A gorgeous sound. Before Drums, the final minute of Terrapin is exciting.

Encore: Casey Jones, one of seven renditions this year.

It's all really good. Masterful work on Market Street.

Link to recordings

### 1982 PALO ALTO, CA
# STANFORD UNIVERSITY, FROST AMPHITHEATER

Their first visit to the campus since 2/9/73. A relatively ordinary-looking setlist for this period is infused with crackling energy.

Set two starts with two of the new ones. Throwing Stones (#7) opens with Weir's urgent earnestness, then it's a smooth change into Touch Of Grey (#6). Garcia's two solo runs are lucid, fast hands on his fills. There's at least one recording where you can hear the crowd going wild on the final "we will survive" chorus.

Estimated Prophet has a great finish to the inside jam. Garcia points the way home (4:14–), followed by some nifty drumming. Weir ramps up his chopping (4:26–) and they begin what should be the final four runs before the next verse. But no! Garcia blasts out into single-note soloing once again (4:59–).

During the exit jam, Garcia sounds some Other One licks (9:40–) but turns back and they find their way into Eyes Of The World. He seems to be thinking in sentences here (see 2/3/78), a wonderful version. The final half minute is Weir, Bill, and Mickey.

Drums and Space is a worthy mid-concert, musical palette cleanser. Towards the end of Space, Garcia again makes Other One noises, but here comes Truckin'. Weir retells the woe that befell sweet Jane: "she took all that dope and had her head rearranged." Garcia leads the rise, a rocket ship with hypersonic riffing. The final three minutes of Truckin' has Other One jamming, Garcia and Weir create a tiptoeing duet right before Lesh's rumbling takeoff.

Morning Dew is a killer. Wear a helmet for the inside break. Both Weir and Garcia brandish their trilled chords during the finale.

The first set is also laden with charms. During On The Road Again, one of seven this year, Weir plays slide licks at times. They'd only perform this great song twice more. Weir's enthusiasm (or the song length) gets him the next lead vocal as well, Beat It On Down The Line, featuring another ad-lib: "Well this job I got, is a little too hot (just like a Swiss watch)." Listen for Garcia's neat little turnaround lick mid-solo (1:47), occasionally employed on other songs throughout his career.

Deadbase respondents in 1991 ranked this concert third best of 1982, tied with the next night. By 1997, it had slipped to tenth place, behind several August concerts. They ranked Touch Of Grey tied for fifth best along with the next night's version, though it's likely even better than that (the respondents' number one version of Touch Of Grey is 12/15/86, the band's first post-coma performance).

Link to recordings

**1983 GREENSBORO, NC**

# GREENSBORO COLISEUM

The band heads 202 miles south for a Sunday gig. They get off to a fast start with a Shakedown Street opener, Garcia's soloing rocking hard during the jam, followed by a rare first set appearance for Samson & Delilah (it was placed in the initial frame four other times in the '80s).

There's superlative soloing on Peggy-O. Garcia's voice is a bit strained, but his fingers still dance like youngsters. The presence of Big Railroad Blues in a set sometimes indicates Garcia wants to cut the rug. Here we get an amazing twelve runs on his second solo, the last few a great surprise.

Let It Grow closes the set, a generally sparkling, fifteen-minute version. Brent begins to come through in the jam after 8:30, and they make the turn a minute later. Garcia then stumbles a bit over the guitar lines leading back to the verse, and Weir seems to miss his cue for the "what shall we say" vocal, rare miscues on this song.

Set two, Garcia starts Eyes Of The World at race car speeds, assisted by the drummers. He trips over his entry into the first verse but keeps barreling ahead and somehow stays on the track.

The following Women Are Smarter also gets off to what seems a forced, frenzied start, but you've got to love the brash energy. This song, like Iko Iko, was always putty in Garcia's hands. Post-Space, an interesting intro to Not Fade Away, Garcia throwing in some extra chords and Brent adding twinkling notes.

Sugar Magnolia closes, Weir rephrases a line: "*knew* she had to come up; soon for air" After the initial verses, Garcia absolutely rips into his solo. What a jolt! During the main break, you'll hear some of Weir's loudest whammying ever (5:00–).

Encore: It's All Over Now, Baby Blue ("this one's for the Dodgers"*
–BW), Garcia is still displaying the Midas touch on his guitar, passionate
screams and whispers on the vocals.

Underrated. A fine night for The Other Man In Black. Show us the SBD.
Our kingdom for a Matrix.

Link to recordings

*October 8, 1983, the series-ending NLCS Game Four. Phillies 7, Dodg-
ers 2.

## 1984 WORCESTER, MA

# THE CENTRUM

Second night here, an inspired six-song start to set two: Help → Slipknot! → Franklin's to open, followed by Jack Straw (its last appearance
in the second half was 3/21/81). After He's Gone, they launch their first
Smokestack Lightning since 1972.

Paired with an all-Chuck Berry close, and a Beatles' encore, perhaps it's
a nod to a notable birthday boy (John Lennon).

On He's Gone, Garcia's vocals are particularly gravelly but infused with
passion ("dogs in a pow-ow-ownd; nothing left to do but smile, smile,
smi-ile"). You'll hear especially spirited "nothin' gonna bring him back"
vocals from both Garcia and Weir.

Already forty minutes and five songs into the set, nobody would fault
them for departing for Drums. But they have something else in mind,
the old Chester Burnett chestnut, Smokestack Lightning. A great surprise, and well done.

Space briefly becomes a Garcia soliloquy of classical music lines (2:30–). Some grotesquely twisted blues phrases emerge after the five-minute mark. The single notes seem suited to entering The Wheel, and that's where they go.

On Throwing Stones, Garcia's unexpected licks between Weir's final vocal lines ("shipping powders back and forth") are followed by a vocal muff, but Weir recovers nicely, finding his place in the lyrics and the song's passionate center.

There's more fine singing and playing on Stella Blue, with a unique rebuild in the final minute of the exit jam. Around And Around gives Brent a chance to shine. On Johnny B. Goode, he launches his solo with some scat singing.

Encore: Revolution (#5).

This performance made the Deadbase respondents' 1984 top ten in 1991, but six years later dropped into the bottom of their top twenty.

Link to recordings

### 1989 HAMPTON, VA
## HAMPTON COLISEUM

Yes, Virginia, there is a Santa Claus.

This is their first Dark Star since 7/13/84, and their first Attics of My Life since 1972. Garcia has the Wolf guitar in tow for another night.

The magic begins with the start of set two and the opening Playing In The Band. Seven minutes of jamming, with throaty, MIDI-flute around the six-minute mark before a lane change into Uncle John's Band, and then a return to finish Playin'.

What's next? Not your typical ballad.

And before you have time to rub your eyes in disbelief, Garcia sings verse one of Dark Star.

Eighteen minutes of exploration follow. Around 5:15, there are some sounds usually heard during Drums. Garcia soon pulls out his MIDI bassoon, and by seven minutes he's making Other One noises.

He picks up the Dark Star theme again around ten minutes and we get verse two. Brent then takes them down the rabbit hole and we're not in Kansas anymore. They enter an unholy matrimony of musical miasma. It's the devil in the key of beware. There are dragons, and then there are Drums.

An interesting Space, and a perfect segue into Death Don't Have No Mercy (see 9/29/89 for their first one in nearly twenty years). It sounds so powerful and rich, it's a wonder it sat on the shelf so long. The song seems as thirsty as a dry sponge for Garcia's late '80s guitar effects and his older, wiser voice. It's a fine vehicle for Brent as well, a fit for his natural blues voice and organ solo.

Encore: Attics Of My Life, a revival with a high degree of difficulty, perhaps a testament to the confidence they now have in their ensemble singing, and in their fellowship.

Deadbase respondents say this is the best of 1989, and given the views/downloads, it seems most fans would agree.

Link to recordings

1994 LANDOVER, MD

## USAIR ARENA

The start of three here, including their first Comes A Time in a year and a half (it turned out to be their last).

In the first set, listen for Vince's contributions; every tune seems to have some nice bits (Spoonful, Stagger Lee, and particularly Broken Arrow). Me & My Uncle has tinkly, western saloon piano, and on Big River he gets a solo that enables him to stretch out.

There seems to be some decent guitar from Garcia in this set (e.g., on the opening Hell In A Bucket), but he seems low in the mix and his lines are hard to hear. So Many Roads has a great vocal finale.

Set two: Way To Go Home is a high point, Garcia's guitar lines here seem energized (the instrumental break is reminiscent of his work on Road Runner in the Jerry Garcia Band). Ship Of Fools is similarly joyous, despite the muffed vocals. They keep it rolling with Saint Of Circumstance; during the exit jam of three minutes they come down from on high and keep jamming.

Post-Space, Comes A Time, Garcia is in good voice for this period.

Link to recordings

# OCTOBER 10

1968 San Francisco, CA, The Matrix
   (Mickey and the Heartbeats)

1970 Flushing, NY, Queens College (CUNY), Colden Auditorium

1976 Oakland, CA, Oakland Coliseum

1980 San Francisco, CA, Warfield Theater

1981 Bremen, Germany, Stadthalle Bremen

1982 Palo Alto, CA, Stanford University, Frost Amphitheater

1994 Landover, MD, USAir Arena

## 1968 SAN FRANCISCO, CA

# THE MATRIX

Mickey and the Heartbeats (no Weir, no Pigpen). Over two and a half hours of music, including jams around Lovelight, Dark Star, The Eleven, and The Seven.

The initial track starts with a So What-type of jazz head. Or perhaps it's the head for Bird Song, transposed. Or perhaps it's a Good Lovin' head. For awhile, Garcia plays rhythm and Phil solos. It starts to run out of gas after fifteen minutes, but at 19:35–20:30 you might think you're hearing Garcia pick out a Fire On The Mountain precursor. Eventually, you'll hear some Alligator riffing.

Link to recordings

## 1970 FLUSHING, NY

# QUEENS COLLEGE (CUNY), COLDEN AUDITORIUM

Their first Goin' Down The Road Feelin' Bad*, albeit without vocals, and only two minutes worth, sandwiched inside Not Fade Away.

On the first portion of Not Fade Away, you'll hear Weir take over the lead guitar duties (3:57–). Garcia rejoins around 5:25, and he soon pencils out a start to Goin' Down The Road.

Set one has what might be their sixth Truckin'. Not much Pigpen lead singing on these recordings except for Hard To Handle, but you can hear what seems to be his keyboard work in various places (e.g., on Me & My Uncle).

Link to recordings

*Going Down The Road Feeling Bad, known by various names since the 1920s, e.g. Lonesome Road Blues by Henry Whitter (1924).

### 1976 OAKLAND, CA

## OAKLAND COLISEUM

"All right without any further to-do, on a nice Sunday morning, The Grateful Dead." –BG

Another brunch gig for the band, this one features two sandwiches. The first is Dancin' In The Streets with Wharf Rat in the middle to end set one. The second comes in set two: Playing In The Band wrapping Drums, The Wheel, Space, The Other One, and Stella Blue.

Dancin' In The Streets has a great jam, by eleven minutes they've left the song far behind and where they're going is anybody's choice. Garcia pulls out his slide after twelve minutes. They finally pick a place to go, and grandly pivot into a first set Wharf Rat (they wouldn't play it again in the first frame until 1987). A wonderful version.

Then they slip right back into Dancin' to end the set. Weir announces his usual, "We're gonna take a break," while they are still strumming.

In set two, after The Wheel we get several minutes of Space, Garcia in full, whirling, psychedelic kaleidoscope mode. They yield to the drummers for a minute before launching The Other One. A propulsive, powerful version, the Spanish lady comes after two minutes. They never let up, rocking all the way into the lily fields verse.

There's a beautiful transition from Stella Blue into whatever is coming next. Within thirty seconds, it starts to feel like a close kin to Slipknot! Then Bill and Mickey pull on the reins and steer the team back into Playing In The Band.

Encore: A boisterous Johnny B. Goode ("thank you and good afternoon." –BW).

Link to recordings

## 1980 SAN FRANCISCO, CA
## WARFIELD THEATER

Twelfth of fifteen on this stand. Heaven.

The acoustic set is its usual sublime self. For those who missed the Grateful Dead in 1970, rejoice. "We're the warm-up band." –BW

Set two, Garcia hits the note several times in Franklin's Tower, particularly on his last solo. Althea summons a sinfully rich, gorgeous sound. His final solo on the song ends with a swashbuckling display of chords. Then comes the set-ending Jack Straw, vigorous soloing, fourteen runs on the outro (notable fireworks on the first, sixth, and tenth runs, among others).

The third set has a strong sextet of songs before Drums, ballads begone. Scarlet Begonias opens and has an extra solo passage after the "look at it right" verse. After returning to the "let her pass by" verse, we then get the main solo.

There's not much to the Scarlet outro jam, and only a very short middle solo in Fire On The Mountain after the "almost abaze" verse. But the exit solo finds Garcia trilling chords, a nice surprise.

At the end of the twenty-minute Drums → Space, Weir sounds a little Dark Starish lick, but after a remote whistle they move into Truckin'. In the final two minutes they fall into a Nobody's Fault But Mine jam, their first in over a year.

The concert has an all-Chuck Berry close. When they end Around And Around, Garcia breaks into the usual Johnny B. Goode intro, but it becomes the launch for Promised Land, the only time they played it to end set two (it was also the tail end of the double encore for 12/11/79). It's a barnburner.

Link to recordings


## 1981 BREMEN, GERMANY
## STADTHALLE BREMEN

After a day off, they cross the Baltic Sea and spend their Saturday night in West Germany.

The first set stretches nearly ninety minutes, with many up-tempo numbers. Near the end of the set, Bird Song conjures an interesting journey. As it nears six minutes, Brent leans chromatic to dissonant while Garcia holds to his happier key. Around 7:30, Garcia repeatedly restates the theme (eventually Brent joins), but rather than signaling the finish, they take off for points unknown. Some pretty notes around the nine-minute mark, they return to the vocals at 10:25.

The set two Sugaree has an exhilarating second solo, Garcia spinning like a turbocharged top (6:23–), then splitting the universe at the peak. Eyes Of The World is a flat-out sprint, with pulse-racing soloing, likely too fast even for speed freaks.

During Space, after the four-minute mark, you'll hear the sound of a bow scraping across a bass. Around 6:45 in Truckin', the jam begins to cross into Other One territory, and they do both verses, with some great organ from Brent.

Encore: Casey Jones.

Some fine playing here and there, listeners would benefit from a better recording.

Link to recordings

## 1982 PALO ALTO, CA

# STANFORD UNIVERSITY, FROST AMPHITHEATER

Sunday afternoon, a couple of new ones are played in set two for the second straight day (Touch Of Grey and Throwing Stones). And there's a double encore.

Weir contributes a notable vocal performance, including an avalanche of ad-libs, a couple of f-bombs, and voting advice. Towards the end of the first set, here he is on Looks Like Rain: "They say into each life a little rain must fall. In my life, it's coming down like a big gray wall."

They close the set with China Cat Sunflower → I Know You Rider. A fabulous transition jam, Weir's slashing chords a perfect crosscut to Garcia's lines (3:55–). Some nuanced jewels appear, like Brent's tiny lines after Weir's "sun will shine" verse. And a righteous rave-up from Garcia at the end of the final jam. Well done.

The set two opening Playing In The Band ends after seven minutes, kind of a shame but no hardship when Crazy Fingers follows. That jam begins around 6:30. Garcia starts angelic, then turns dark and Moorish, before heading back to the heavenly theme.

Around the nine-minute mark, they bid goodbye to the song and create something brand new. It quickly sounds like they're not sure where to go, and Garcia nibbles early on Lost Sailor. Weir tells the faithful like it is, a veritable Sermon On The Frost: "Free don't come easy, free don't always come for free. Don't always know what to believe in, sometimes you're just driftin' now. Don't know who to be, what to be. So you trust your luck now. Driftin' and dreamin'…"

On Saint Of Circumstance, the inside jam, Garcia begins raunchy, then makes his assault on the mountain, dancing wildly at the peak, Weir planting his vocal flag: "Well I never know, guess you don't either now…just exactly what the f-ck you gonna do now?"

Touch Of Grey (#7) follows, interesting to hear it a second straight day, but here the solo is less lucid. They end it and Garcia continues to pick and wander, perhaps he's game for a sixth song pre-Drums, but it's not to be.

Post-Space, after The Wheel we get Throwing Stones (#8), also played last night, Garcia hits higher peaks on this solo. They close with Sugar Magnolia, Weir pausing before Sunshine Daydream to remind the crowd, "Don't forget to vote Yes on 12 if you can vote."

Double encore: Satisfaction and Baby Blue, excellent, followed by Bill Graham stage announcements: "Hope to god they like us and we like you and you like us we'll be back here sometime next year hopefully."

Deadbase respondents in '97 ranked this concert second best of '82, one vote behind 4/19/82. Headyversion voters rank this Sailor → Saint version best ever, by a wide margin (they also rate Baby Blue best, Looks Like Rain second best, and Cassidy tied for second best, all-time).

Link to recordings

## 1994 LANDOVER, MD
# USAIR ARENA

The middle concert here, they feel like partying on a Monday night and open with Iko Iko. The six-song first set closes with Eternity, a somewhat interesting jam, with a nod to The Other One, briefly, around 7:30.

Set two is perhaps ample reward for sticking around, a solid '70s repertoire pre-Drums, opening with Help → Slipknot! → Franklin's.

Garcia holds his own during Slipknot! He switches to chords near what might seem the end, but Bill and Mickey kick it up and they're going to tango on for another three minutes. Garcia warbles (4:45–), then begins a relaxed rise before returning to the Slipknot! theme. They stumble a bit to get over the finish line and into Franklin's Tower, but a fine late-era effort.

Fifteen minutes of Franklin's ensues. They give it a long intro; the first verse comes near the four-minute mark. A perky version, testimony to Bill and Mickey's propulsion. Without skipping a beat, they enter Estimated Prophet, Weir in high spirits.

Terrapin Station goes ten minutes and then a new jam begins. It has momentum, like a Supplication jam does. Always a good sign to hear them still exploring after five songs in the second set.

Link to recordings

# OCTOBER 11

1968 San Francisco, CA, Avalon Ballroom
(no setlist, no recording)

1970 Wayne, NJ, Paterson State College, Marion Shea Auditorium

1977 Norman, OK, University of Oklahoma, Lloyd Noble Center

1980 San Francisco, CA, Warfield Theater

1981 Amsterdam, The Netherlands, The Melkweg
(Garcia & Weir only)

1983 New York City, NY, Madison Square Garden

1984 Augusta, ME, Augusta Civic Center

1989 East Rutherford, NJ, Brendan Byrne Arena

1994 Landover, MD, USAir Arena

1970 WAYNE, NJ

## PATERSON STATE COLLEGE, MARION SHEA AUDITORIUM

Likely their second ever Goin' Down The Road, this one has words. The singing starts at 1:45. Like last night's rendition, it's sandwiched amidst two slices of Not Fade Away.

You've got to love the 1966-style Dancing in the Street sound, with Weir's lead and the harmony vocals. Also on the bill, Till The Morning Comes (#3, as far as we know).

We also have a twenty-minute Dark Star, one of twenty-two they performed in 1970; the first verse comes at 4:08. At 13:40, Garcia finds a theme and they drive it down the tracks. He restates the head (15:56 and 18:35), and then we get verse two (19:00).

Link to recordings

1977 NORMAN, OK

## UNIVERSITY OF OKLAHOMA, LLOYD NOBLE CENTER

The band visits the 46th state for the first time in four years.

Lesh gets them off to a fine start with the high, lonesome bass notes of Help On The Way. They stumble a bit getting into Slipknot!, and Franklin's Tower feels a bit sluggish at times. Halfway through, Garcia does find a nice phrase (7:40−), and there's some excitement when he goes to chords near the end (11:25−) and Bill and Mickey start to gallop. After this performance, they'd shelve Help and Slipknot! until 3/25/83.

On Jack Straw, the outro jam is short. Garcia takes eleven runs, the first three are all chords. Listen for Bill and Mickey's flourishes at the end of the fifth and eighth runs.

Let It Grow closes set one; it's a great version, like several from Fall '77 through Winter/Spring '78. Amidst the first jam, Garcia soars, then they make the slight turn (4:35–) and Bill and Mickey have a supercharged moment. At the start of the "I am" jam (7:40–), Garcia warbles like a disturbed Amazonian bird.

Set two, Estimated Prophet, the exit jam is the ticket. Garcia pushes his Mu-Tron to the max, a classic '77 tone, while the rhythm section rivals the best jazz combos. They concoct a smooth segue into Eyes Of The World.

During Not Fade Away, much of the jam consists of raga-like mantras coming from Garcia. Around the twelve-minute mark, they break into a section of trading fours, Garcia tossing phrases back and forth with Keith, Lesh squeezing phrases in between. Later, the drummers break out into a rollicking pattern (14:45); it's anything from Caution to Big River. Who knows where they are headed?

The destination turns out to be the docks of the city. An exquisite sound at the start; when Garcia begins to sing it feels like you haven't heard from him in ages.

Link to recordings

## 1980 SAN FRANCISCO, CA
## WARFIELD THEATER

The band's thirteenth performance at this venue in seventeen days. John Cipollina joins several songs at the end of set three.

The acoustic set is another cloud nine. On Rosalie McFall, Brent's speedy lines are on display. Cassidy begets Garcia's rousing solo.

Feel Like A Stranger opens the first electric set. The Fall '80 versions of this song were crisp and punchy. This one features a variety of funky Brent keyboard sounds and Weir's punctuating chords. Garcia is great deep in the jam; after seven minutes, his howling, feedbacking bends reintroduce the theme.

Later in the set, Brent sings the lead lines in Passenger along with Weir, Garcia's second solo here has some interesting peaks. He delivers additional excitement on the set-closing Saint Of Circumstance.

The final set has a good Let It Grow pre-Drums, Garcia blasting off with his first solo.

They expertly revert to the main theme at 7:40. After the ten-minute mark, there are some notable licks from Weir; then they fingerpaint the theme before a long unwinding into Drums.

Deadbase respondents ranked this tenth best on the year, but well behind 10/10/80 on this stand.

Link to recordings

1981 AMSTERDAM, THE NETHERLANDS

## THE MELKWEG

Garcia and Weir travel from West Germany to the Netherlands (356 kilometers) and serenade the crowd with seven songs.

Link to recordings

 1983 NEW YORK CITY, NY

## MADISON SQUARE GARDEN

St. Stephen returns! (see 1/10/79). The pre-Drums section alone qualifies this concert as one of the best of the year (and perhaps the decade), well before fortune comes a crawlin' out of Space.

Set two has a China Cat → Rider opener, Garcia's soloing is snappy from the start. There's a full eight minutes and a half before they begin the I Know You Rider vocals.

An indication of their energy on this night: they skip a seemingly obligatory set two ballad and after a thirty-second intermezzo move into I Need A Miracle → Bertha. The final thirty seconds of Miracle has a unique little jam. There's no hint of Bertha until Garcia forcefully changes up the chords. An up-tempo version, they keep galloping.

Bertha ends, and they invent a brand-new jam out of thin air (listen for Lesh's high notes, among other things). Great!

China Doll is next, Brent's harpsichord sound recalling 1969 and Aoxomoxoa. An extended exit jam.

Drums and Space are worth a listen. Persistent xylophone sounds, wood blocks, and percolating percussion. Then Space begins with Garcia's low register alien visitor sounds, and later, Weir's Sage & Spirit-like picking (3:25–) (see also 10/21/83). By six minutes, Garcia is hitting low notes that drip like a scene from a Salvador Dali painting.

St. Stephen is an epic surprise, perhaps even for those who heard the sound check (see 10/9/83), and quite good considering the nearly five-year layoff. There's a decent inside jam and a clean return to the vocals. The answer to The Answer Man is a revisit of the earlier jam, but then a difficult, stumbling transition that finally reaches Throwing Stones.

"Don't ever underestimate the heart of a champion." RT

Deadbase X ('97) rated this numero uno by a fairly wide margin (the earlier poll ranked 9/11/83 one vote higher).

Link to recordings

## 1984 AUGUSTA, ME
## AUGUSTA CIVIC CENTER

First of two nights here. The centerpiece is the pre-Drums, fourteen-minute Playing In The Band that they finish the next night.

Particularly expressive playing from Garcia early, especially on the Greatest Story that follows the opening Shakedown Street. Rambunctious. Yes, his vocals are mid-'80s strained, but they're paired with his continued ability to explore the fretboard like no other.

On Mama Tried, he takes four runs on his solo, double the usual load. Big River has some nice work from Brent. Ramble On Rose lends itself well to Garcia's gravelly voice, perhaps giving the song additional gravitas. They close the set with Might As Well, Brent sprinkling Jerry Lee Lewis flourishes.

Set two, Playing In The Band, Weir completely muffs the lyrics right from the start, oh well. The jam slows a bit around the six-minute mark, and they kind of clear the decks a minute later. There's some avant-garde chording from Weir (7:55–) and Garcia's Dark Star-like sounds (10:15–). Then they get old-style wiggy, building a cacophony that will take you into a musical wormhole.

Hang around for Drums, a heart-racing mix of sticks and tones.

Link to recordings

## 1989 EAST RUTHERFORD, NJ
# BRENDAN BYRNE ARENA

The day after the day after Dark Star, they hunker down for five nights in New Jersey.

Night one, not so great. Set one is particularly troubled with mumbled lyrics and uninspired soloing. They close the set with Just A Little Light and Don't Ease Me In.

When I Paint My Masterpiece has its moments, though it starts with sluggish to nonexistent fills from Garcia. Weir garishly growls, "It sure has been a long hard ride," then stretches the following Dylan lyric like a rubber band. He holds the final "when I paint" forever, then runs it out of bounds. Yikes.

Set two, China Cat Sunflower is sluggish out of the gate. A tentative jam, Garcia sounds the nine-note peak (5:13) but then pulls back. Truly uninspired. Around 7:15, it suddenly becomes a Weir and Drums-led jam, then Garcia turns on his MIDI, then off, then on. Ugh.

I Know You Rider is no better. Garcia can barely get the notes out of his guitar before Weir's "sun will shine" verse. On the final sung chorus, you can hear how out of synch they are. On Estimated Prophet, Weir continues an odd mix of sung and spoken lines that are perhaps strange even for him.

Terrapin Station goes pretty well, until the band completely flubs the "inspiration" turn.

Not recommended.

Link to recordings


## 1994 LANDOVER, MD
# USAIR ARENA

Third of three here, the first set is more compelling than the second. A more typical 1994 performance than the Boston Garden gigs.

The Picasso Moon opener's energy is welcome, like its kissin' cousin Hell In A Bucket. Jack A Roe finds Garcia singing decently. It's All Over Now has a good beat; Vince's honky-tonk piano solo is a bright spot, he takes two runs, finishing with a rockabilly flourish.

The first few notes of High Time bring a big roar of recognition from the crowd. Garcia is in surprisingly good voice for such a challenging chart, though he has occasional trouble recalling some lines.

If The Shoe Fits offers some good possibilities for jamming. But in late '94, Garcia doesn't quite have the chops to rip it up. The following Lazy River Road is more up his alley at this point in his career, channeling Elizabeth Cotten.

Easy Answers is an up-tempo Weir bookend for Picasso Moon. Deal closes the set; after six minutes the jam begins to gel, then some Vince sounds come through (6:55). But there's not much power here.

Set two: skip ahead to the twenty-minute Drums → Space. The Eyes Of The World opener is nada y nada y nada. No builds, no magic. By 13:45, what's the point of continuing with this? It sounds like six guys standing around waiting for somebody to say something. Sad.

For those with the patience or courage to stick around, you'll get their first China Doll in over a year. It's still a beautiful song, sung by its quintessential interpreter. The tempo is a bit fast during the final sung chorus and the short, but lovely, exit jam.

Weir's closing Sugar Magnolia injects some energy into a set sorely missing it, Bill and Mickey bashing in kind.

Link to recordings

# OCTOBER 12

1968 San Francisco, CA, Avalon Ballroom

1977 Austin, TX, Manor Downs

1981 Munich, Germany, Olympia Halle

1983 New York City, NY, Madison Square Garden

1984 Augusta, ME, Augusta Civic Center

1989 East Rutherford, NJ, Brendan Byrne Arena

## 1968 SAN FRANCISCO, CA
## AVALON BALLROOM

"OK, we're gonna do a elementary dance number now; it's a foxtrot and it's also a ladies choice."

That's Weir introducing a classic Dark Star like the one on *Live Dead*: museum quiet, maracas shaking, Garcia's notes shining like stars in the night sky. We later get unidentified percussion sounds (8:30–) (guiro?).

During St. Stephen, there's a great ad-lib from Weir after the "one man gathers" line ("funniest thing I ever heard"). Garcia's fills are lively; it's a shame there is no extended jam. The Eleven displays Garcia's early genius, stunning lines. Listen to the power of the band's two-drummer attack. Somehow, they motor down from supersonic to slow blues in less than fifteen seconds.

A jaw-dropping forty minutes of music. And there's more. But no Pigpen tonight.

Link to recordings

## 1977 AUSTIN, TX
## MANOR DOWNS

The band travels 368 miles south from Oklahoma for a night gig at this horse racing facility on the outskirts of Austin. Set two is the place to start. It includes their first Nobody's Fault But Mine in three years (7/29/74), and a simple Iko Iko (#3) before the closing Sugar Magnolia.

Samson & Delilah starts that set, Garcia's soloing driven and focused. Keith nearly gets a solo (4:50–), but Garcia quickly overrides and goes into higher gear, driving the drummers to match him.

Out of Drums, The Other One starts to wind down around 8:45 and they noodle around for quite some time, down to a whisper of tones from Garcia, Lesh, and Weir. Where to?

Black Peter is next. During the "run and see" jam (9:05–), the tempo is swinging and swaying like church—you can imagine Ray Charles having a field day with this. Garcia pushes it through the roof (11:40) and later fashions some terrific double-noted growls.

On Truckin', after reaching the initial peak in the jam, Garcia starts a rousing second build (6:19–) and Bill, Mickey, and Lesh join to drive it to a massive peak. Then there's an interesting transition to whatever's coming next.

Weir starts a pattern that is nothing like where they end up. It's not until Garcia finally picks out the melody (2:48) that you're sure it's Nobody's Fault But Mine. He seals it by singing a single verse. Don't blink, the next one isn't until 1/5/79.

From there, it's an easier shuffling segue into Iko Iko, then Sugar Magnolia to close.

Set one: try Friend Of The Devil, a great ensemble soundscape.

Link to recordings

## 1981 MUNICH, GERMANY
# OLYMPIA HALLE

Garcia and Weir get back on the bus and return to West Germany from the Netherlands, a change of countries traversing 830 kilometers.

In set one, Garcia's final solo on Mexicali Blues is a good one, fast and articulate. They close the set with China Cat Sunflower, a strong start, solid tempo, Garcia phrasing melodically throughout the jam. I Know You Rider has more of the same in the jam before the "sun gonna shine" verse.

During Estimated Prophet in set two, you can clearly hear Lesh's odd, sliding lines before Weir starts singing. The inside jam kind of goes sideways until Garcia goes high for his final four runs. An exciting finish, but they don't exactly stick the landing, with Garcia's rogue notes winging like errant kites as Weir returns to the vocal.

A long exit jam follows, Garcia restates the main Estimated theme (9:50–), and they keep on going. Around twelve minutes, it quiets down to the drummers, picking up steam again in the final minute.

There's an interesting segue into Goin' Down The Road with some throaty organ from Brent at the start. But Garcia's first run feels rushed and awkward. On the second run, he switches on a muddy effect, even worse. The third run is high speed, much brighter (2:30–), but it sounds like he's really forcing it.

He takes several more, then four after the final verse. The pace is so amped up, they can't pull off the Bid You Goodnight coda. Instead, it's a wandering transition into Brent's blues, Good Times (Never Trust A Woman) (#7). They end that tune, and Garcia goes off on a speedy soliloquy before Bill and Mickey take over for Drums.

Not Fade Away has a six-minute intro that is not compelling. But after the second verse, there's a sudden burst of energy from Garcia. It quickly fades, with nearly two minutes of low-key wandering before they get to Stella Blue.

The Stella exit jam has a melodic build, Garcia weaving around six notes (9:35–), some of his best stuff on the night. About 11:30, he pulls back on the reins rather than hitting a peak, with just enough braking to enter Around And Around.

Link to recordings

## 1983 NEW YORK CITY, NY
# MADISON SQUARE GARDEN

The day after St. Stephen, there's still some gas left in the tank. They'll unveil their new Beatles cover as an encore.

The concert opens with a hot Cold Rain & Snow. After the "faithful tune" verse, Garcia double tongues a bit, Bill and Mickey catch it and try to encourage him. Garcia keeps it up, doubling down even while singing the next verse. Unique.

On the set two opener Help On The Way, Lesh's second line has sky-high notes. There's a bit of a glitch getting into Slipknot! but the jam heats up three minutes in. A long version, it has a quirky end featuring a long coda from Garcia.

Franklin's Tower has a two-minute intro, and the third solo's the charm. Near the end, Garcia plays a rising lick that is kin to Foolish Heart

(13:15–13:30). His guitar is generally quick and snappy throughout, as well as on the following Women Are Smarter.

He's Gone has just a two-minute jam before Drums; the descending line and slinky tempo would be a fine fit for Cosmic Charlie.

Encore: Revolution (#1).

Link to recordings

## 1984 AUGUSTA, ME

# AUGUSTA CIVIC CENTER

An interesting set one song list, and they finish off last night's Playing In The Band. Well played, top to bottom.

Great jamming on the opening Feel Like A Stranger (anybody who thinks they were washed up in '84, listen here and think twice). It Must Have Been The Roses is promoted to the second spot. Then another surprise, On The Road Again, performed just once in 1983 (this one turned out to be their last). Jack A Roe is next, their first in two and a half years. What's got into them tonight?

The closing Music Never Stopped ends with a whimper. Or does it? At 7:30, it seems to be over, but they have other things in mind. But no trilled chords.

Set two: Uncle John's Band has near constant speedy soloing from Garcia, a frenetic to frantic pace. Around 10:30, they finally slow it down, then toss a musical coin with six sides; where will it land? A new jam is born, a stroll through the stars until Drums.

During Drums → Space, Garcia sounds the Playing In The Band theme around eleven minutes in, but the rest of the band stays largely quiet, remaining in Space mode. Bill and Mickey are the first to fall in line. They bring it all the way back, Weir launching into the vocals and finishing what they started last night (Deadbase says this is the first "Playin Reprise").

From there, it's back to the D minor jam in Uncle John's Band, along with the vocals, then Morning Dew. Passionately sung, the inside break gets a brief bit of Garcia's trilled chords. The final break begins with some oddly pained, poignant bends. There are clusters of descending four-note phrases, then a gorgeous gossamer bend near the top of his fretboard.

Encore: Good Lovin', Weir gives it a little extra ("Jerry's gonna tell ya about it").

Deadbase respondents say this is a top ten concert for 1984. Headyversion voters say Morning Dew is sixth best all-time.

Link to recordings

## 1989 EAST RUTHERFORD, NJ

# BRENDAN BYRNE ARENA

Marginally better than last night. Set two does have a setlist resembling 1972, but for the opener.

Set one: on Bird Song, Garcia begins the break with a fuzzy flute; then you'll hear xylophone overtones. Later, it's something like a synthed French café accordion. The jam peaks around 9:20, then they continue to explore. It's back to the vocals after the twelve-minute mark.

Queen Jane has some sparkly stuff from Brent, one of the few highlights. On the closing Jack Straw, the final jam, Garcia gets off to a slow start, and his guitar seems low in the mix (though there are some nice licks from Brent).

The next set has two fast ones then two slow ones before Drums. The opening Hey Pocky Way has Brent singing lead, and he also gets the first solo. On Cumberland Blues, Weir starts singing the final verse—"lotta poor man"—but it's Garcia's line so he backs off.

Looks Like Rain is kind of a cartoon version of its former self. He's Gone has no real exit jam after the finishing group vocals.

Post-Space, there are some creative sounds in The Other One. After winding down Wharf Rat, they seem to have trouble starting Sugar Magnolia. Not a great version.

Link to recordings

# OCTOBER 13

1968 San Francisco, CA, Avalon Ballroom

1980 San Francisco, CA, Warfield Theater

1981 Russelheim, Germany, Walter Kobel Halle

1989 NBC Studios
   (Garcia & Weir only)

1990 Stockholm, Sweden, Ice Stadium

1994 New York City, NY, Madison Square Garden

1968 SAN FRANCISCO, CA

## AVALON BALLROOM

Second straight night here. It's the same setlist, but this one is missing the extra jam between New Potato Caboose and Drums.

Dark Star, an early version, all the musical tent poles are in place, thirteen minutes of that wonderful weave of bass, rhythm, and lead guitar lines.

It takes them about twelve seconds to descend from warp speed to slow blues, courtesy of their psychedelic-hydraulic brake system. Garcia's Death Don't Have No Mercy run starting at 5:15 is truly innovative, going perhaps where no blues solo had gone before.

As you keep listening to Cryptical Envelopment, The Other One, and the rest, it becomes clear that the band were early creators of what came to be called "prog rock", given the long improvisations, complex changing chords and time signatures, fantastical lyrics, and classical music motifs (Garcia's peak descending, eight-note line in The Eleven is a traditional theme you can still hear sometimes played on a church bell) (7:43–).

A year later, the country, western, and folk barbarians had scaled the walls of their setlists, as the band shed its skin once again.

Link to recordings

1980 SAN FRANCISCO, CA

## WARFIELD THEATER

"Not only that, folks, it's Bob's wedding anniversary." –PL

More magic on Market Street. The first set has the second acoustic version of El Paso since 1970 (see also 10/7/80). Dig Garcia's trills at 3:30! Bird Song has a sublime acoustic jam.

A solid Sugaree opens set two. And there's a good Supplication jam, yes, like a Swiss watch.

Set three: they start the opening Samson & Delilah with Bill and Mickey, then unveil a funky Jam featuring Garcia and Brent. Weir doesn't start the vocals until 5:29. Unique.

Between The Other One verses, we get a hair-raising solo from Garcia. From there, they stop on a dime, get pin-drop quiet, and tiptoe into Stella Blue. A spirited Johnny B. Goode to close.

Encore: Casey Jones.

A fine performance, deserving of a complete soundboard.

Link to recordings


1981 RUSSELHEIM, GERMANY

## WALTER KOBEL HALLE

A good performance, with an eight-minute Jam after Saint Of Circumstance. Black Peter appears between Sugar Magnolia and Sunshine Daydream.

Start with set two. Lost Sailor floats like a feather, a demonstration of the band's mastery of dynamics. Weir steps back (5:20–5:57) and lets the music play the band, lovely Garcia, Drums, and Brent.

On Saint Of Circumstance, Weir testifies during the final sung chorus ("some folks dream their lives away... they settle for a diamond or a Chevrolet, somethin' like that").

They close the song around the seven-minute mark and begin a brand-new jam. Garcia finds a wonderful repeating pattern and then another; you can feel the DNA of Dark Star in it (the A-G-D chord canvas is close to Dark Star's A-Em-G). Around ten minutes, he drops out and Bill, Mickey, and Brent carry it forward, fabulous keyboard licks.

Space spotlights Garcia for the first three minutes, then we get a scary movie soundtrack. The sound of seabirds (Weir?) leads them into Spanish Jam. A colorful mix of tones and textures, marvelous musical paella, it's better balanced than other versions that are a bit too focused on repetition of the theme.

As The Wheel finishes, Garcia finds the end of the road and the drummers get the bus cranked up. On Sugar Magnolia's main jam, it seems everyone has dropped out by 4:45, leaving just Brent jamming away. Garcia reenters thirty seconds later and we even hear a few notes from Lesh. Then there's a surprise: instead of Sunshine Daydream, we get Black Peter.

Encore: Satisfaction (#8), some great harmony vocals from Brent.

The first set is also well played. Bird Song, Looks Like Rain, even the set-closing Don't Ease Me In shines with Garcia's brilliant ascending runs.

Link to recordings

## 1990 STOCKHOLM, SWEDEN
# ICE STADIUM

After three weeks off, the band crosses the Atlantic Ocean for the first time since 1981 and begins their European tour. It's their first (and only) visit to Sweden. Bruce Hornsby is absent.

Set one: Garcia's singing is decent on Bird Song, and the jam has a compelling repeating run from Vince (5:45–). Lesh's crunchy, seesawing bass is up in the mix throughout, a treat.

Set two: on Estimated Prophet, their first rendition in nearly a month, Weir seems right at home, though they don't quite stick the landing coming out of the inside jam. Vince's playing only hints at the Steely Dan licks he will someday harp on. The outside jam starts to get a bit dissonant (Garcia), and Vince begins to run, but they shut it down to enter Crazy Fingers.

Garcia's vocals are kind of weak here. They wind the Crazy Fingers jam down to the ground where Playing In the Band sounds like a cold start rather than a segue. The upbeat energy is a welcome tonic, but after Weir's first verse, have they (Garcia?) forgotten how to play this part (0:45–)?

The jam as usual fares well, as reliable as Old Faithful. Around the eight-minute mark, they gently kiss the theme and there are hints of an interesting turn in the jam, but they yield to Drums.

Link to recordings

## 1994 NEW YORK CITY, NY

# MADISON SQUARE GARDEN

The first of a six-night stand. A longish first set (nine songs) but a shorter second frame, with just three songs before and after Drums → Space.

They open with Touch Of Grey, plenty of energy here propelled by Lesh, Bill, and Mickey. Some color from Weir's whammy bar and Vince's skating rink tones. Wang Dang Doodle carries a fabulous organ solo from Vince that channels Booker T. and the M.G.'s, on par with what often came out of Brent's rig.

On Loser, Garcia is in surprisingly strong voice. Mama Tried is bright as a new penny. Mexicali Blues has Garcia's MIDI horn sounds fit for Mardi Gras, with Bill and Mickey stoking the party. Vince's honky-tonk saloon licks come later, and Weir returns to the vocals on cue. Nice.

Garcia is still singing with some gusto on Dupree's Diamond Blues. His guitar intro features a quacking Daffy Duck effect. This was recently played (9/24/94) but still sounds like a surprise as it had been out of the repertoire for four years (this turned out to be their last rendition).

Set two: Foolish Heart opens, and Garcia and the drummers start with a shuffle, an easy relaxed tempo. His voice seems to be fading some, but the final sung lines in the last few minutes are vibrant, and the final jam gets off to a strong melodic footing. They wind it all the way down until Weir begins to count off the beats before Playing In The Band.

The Playin' jam is unmistakably Grateful Dead and interesting. There's a hint of running out of gas around 8:55, but Bill and Mickey won't allow it, deciding to drive it harder, until around 10:30 when they decide to slow and consider their options.

Uncle John's Band is where they ride. Twelve minutes into the song, Garcia turns to his MIDI and extends the long D minor exit jam. It retains a loose connection to that theme for awhile, then goes for another six minutes before Drums.

The first four minutes of The Other One track should be considered Space. The Spanish lady comes at 5:30. They do both verses.

The entry into Wharf Rat might remind you of Dark Star if you close your eyes. Not much of a jam, inside or out. Johnny B. Goode sounds like an afterthought.

A pretty good performance for the era but not on par with the recent Boston Garden gigs, and likely benefits from an excellent recording.

Link to recordings

# OCTOBER 14

1966 Palo Alto, CA, Stanford University, TMU Deck
(no setlist, no recording)

1967 Santa Clara, CA, Continental Ballroom
(partial setlist, no recording)

1976 Los Angeles, CA, Shrine Auditorium

1977 Houston, TX, Hofheinz Pavilion

1980 San Francisco, CA, Warfield Theater

1983 Hartford, CT, Hartford Civic Center

1984 Hartford, CT, Hartford Civic Center

1988 Miami, FL, Miami Arena

1989 East Rutherford, NJ, Brendan Byrne Arena

1994 New York City, NY, Madison Square Garden

## 1976 LOS ANGELES, CA
# SHRINE AUDITORIUM

Their first visit to this venue is memorable, especially set two.

Scarlet Begonias ends the first set—listen to those zooming bass licks from Lesh! A fine rendition, the heart-of-gold-band-jam starts at 4:39, Garcia works it to a peak around 7:30, and Lesh is prominent on the next one around 8:15. They pull their lines together to form a slick return to the theme around 9:10. Worth a close listen, deserving of a better recording.

There's more grand stuff from Lesh on the Minglewood Blues set two opener. A lilting Mississippi Half Step follows; it's not yet the full bore rocker it will become, though Garcia ramps up his soloing some on the final jam. Ship Of Fools has pretty piano from Keith throughout. Don't miss this.

Dancin' In The Streets is crisp, Garcia lithe and in full command. Around 8:40, the jam turns slightly darker. Then around 9:55, it slows and spins as they contemplate the possibilities. Lesh throws in some new chords and we briefly get a new theme, while Bill and Mickey take their turn at churning up something different.

Coming out of Wharf Rat there's an interesting modulation that starts around 1:40 in a revived Dancin' jam, Garcia toggling between chords. About a minute later, Weir chimes in, Bill and Mickey chase his tail, and they build a ravenous crescendo before returning to the theme. Great.

Around And Around has an inside break like few others; Garcia goes through the roof and Weir returns to the vocals over the moon. They are clearly feeling it, the heart of rock 'n' roll.

Set one has assorted charms, including Big River with a Bob Wills hoe-down flavor. And there's an interesting Music Never Stopped exit jam; they go with a brief four-chord progression before zeroing in on the classic three-chord stomp (but there's no rave-up at the end).

Encore: Johnny B. Goode, making for a rare Chuck Berry three-fer evening (see also 3/9/73).

Underrated, a sleeper of the vintage. Still the best band in the land.

Link to recordings

## 1977 HOUSTON, TX
# HOFHEINZ PAVILION

Their first gig in this city in five years. "We're trying to get everything just exactly perfect." –BW

Notable is the eighteen-minute front end of Playing In The Band, plus the double encore that finishes it off (Brokedown Palace → Playin'). We also hear the first Jack Straw to ever open a concert.

In set two, Playing In The Band bats cleanup. The jam briefly quiets to drumming around 6:45, but they forge ahead—meandering, percolating, bubbling, a long run of low white water. Later, Garcia utters a forlorn, stuttering staccato call (13:34–) and somehow it sends them down a brand-new road. He uncorks another sparkler (14:54), they quiet, but then rebuild; Weir starts to pounce a bit like on Supplication (16:20–).

A short Drums, the tom-toms are a treat, the right equipment to launch The Wheel. There's a beguiling exit jam, a full two minutes, perhaps a hint of Playin' (5:50), but their actual destination remains a mystery.

Wharf Rat features quite an exit jam; Garcia yearns to break the surly bonds and yes, fly away (8:35–). He comes back down to Earth and makes guitar goose steps on top of Bill and Mickey's march music, then flies off once more. The "got up and wandered" verse arrives at 11:55 with another race to the stars after that. A fine example of the powerful potential of this composition. The drummers downshift skillfully and we get Around And Around to close.

Encore: Brokedown Palace, still a relatively rare selection at this time (it's their fifth and last rendition of the year, all encores; it was not performed in 1976). At the end, you can hear Weir count off to begin a return to Playing In The Band. After the jam, they do the finishing vocals, a great surprise.

Link to recordings

## 1980 SAN FRANCISCO, CA
## WARFIELD THEATER

The final performance of their fifteen-concert stand in twenty days here.

The first electric set has an interesting close (Let It Grow → The Wheel → Music Never Stopped). The second set has an old-school Playing In The Band sandwich, including a Morning Dew. And there's a double encore.

The acoustic set remains a wonder. We get two Garcia solos on All Around This World. China Doll almost sounds like 1973 with its plaintive vocal from Garcia and Brent's harpsichord voicings and trills.

Let It Grow has a surprising wind down that leads not to Deal or "we'll be back in a few minutes" but to The Wheel. They close with Music

Never Stopped. Garcia breaks into his fabled trills a bit early in the final jam (5:50), then Weir raises the stakes, a thrilling series of rising chords.

The final set is well played, each song generally circumscribed in length, a trade-off in exchange for a three-set performance of over thirty songs. On the last instrumental break in Fire On The Mountain, Garcia starts with the classic descending theme then turns on the jets briefly. Estimated Prophet has a short exit jam, quiet, subdued, no barnburner here.

Drums quickly quiets to what sounds like a single bass string, one reverberating tone, like an amplified elephantine piano wire (Lesh?). Four and a half minutes in, we get some skins.

After Space, it's no mere three-song finish as we get I Need A Miracle → Uncle John's Band → Morning Dew → Playin' → Good Lovin'.

Don't blink or you might miss Miracle. There's about thirty seconds worth of exit jam before transitioning to Uncle John's. At the end of that one, there are just four runs of the D minor exit before they start Morning Dew, and it drives the crowd delirious.

Garcia starts the vocals with a whisper; it's their fourth and final performance of the song this year. He builds a skyscraping inside solo and then brings the trills. More whispery vocals, then spine-tingling, roaring riffing. Done?

They have another notion. An unexpected return to Playing In The Band to finish the vocals. All done?

Nope. Send them home with some Good Lovin'.

"Thanks a lot you people are just great." –JG

"The only trouble is you're crazy." –BW

Double encore: U.S. Blues and Brokedown Palace.

Deadbase respondents have this just outside their top ten for the year, with 10/10/80 and 10/11/80 higher.

Link to recordings

 **1983 HARTFORD, CT**

# HARTFORD CIVIC CENTER

The first of two nights here, Garcia has a particularly good evening. In set two, they go big: a thirty-two minute Scarlet → Fire, an eighteen-minute Eyes Of The World, and Spanish Jam out of Space.

Alabama Getaway is the opener, some mumbled lyrics but stirring soloing, especially the final segment. There is plenty of gusto in Garcia's guitar tonight, even in the "ordinary" songs, e.g., Mama Tried. On the final break in Big River, he's so pumped up he solos right over Weir's return to the chorus.

Set two: on Scarlet Begonias, there are unique marimba* sounds before the first verse. Garcia takes five turns on his inside solo; the fourth has a burst of energy. The heart-of-gold-band-jam starts with a hint of the same idiophone, Garcia melodic throughout, finding phrases, unleashing an extended vortex after the eleven-minute mark.

Fire On The Mountain sounds a bit sluggish next to the Scarlet jam, though it has continued expressive soloing, and a noticeable vocal twist: "when your *dreams!* come true-oooh." Garcia hits a huge peak in the second break after 10:35 that thrills the crowd. There's another drive to the top of the mountain on the final break, then restate the Scarlet theme to close (there's that marimba again).

In Eyes Of The World, after the "comes a redeemer" verse and chorus (6:30–), there's a good jam early that seems to fade before finding its big moment. Around the eleven-minute mark, Garcia explodes into a stunning trill, egged on by Bill and Mickey. Worth the wait.

After the final verse, Garcia is still feverishly searching, noodling, and the jam just keeps on going, energy to burn, another six minutes' worth.

Space has low Close Encounters/Jaws-style tones. Around 3:45, if you close your eyes, you might imagine Eugene 1/22/78 (but if you want St. Stephen, you'll have to come back tomorrow night).

It's Weir who first signals Spanish Jam, their fifth of six this year. This one is more like a guitar duo, just Weir and Garcia, nothing from the drummers or Lesh. After three minutes, they go elsewhere, with vague references to The Other One.

A great performance, underrated by respondents in '97 (just five votes), it has since deservedly gained more attention.

Link to recordings

*Xylophone has shorter sustain; probably a keyboard effect; did they have an actual marimba?

**1984 HARTFORD, CT**
# HARTFORD CIVIC CENTER

After taking Saturday night off, they play the first of two here. Set one
has eleven songs—rare for the year—and six songs pre-Drums, with a
long post-Eyes Of The World Jam, perhaps unwittingly pushing the
envelope on the building's curfew (no encore). They close the night with
the newly revived Turn On Your Lovelight (see 7/7/84).

Like last year's opener at this venue, we hear mumbled Alabama Getaway
lyrics followed by impressive soloing. Brent gets the second break, an
exciting second run. On Greatest Story, Garcia plays the bridge for the
"Abraham and Isaac" verse (2:22–), but Weir or his microphone drop
out so it's all instrumental. Listen for the drumming underneath the
first two turns, crisp.

Dupree's Diamond Blues brings Brent's puff organ keyboard sounds.
Garcia's final solo features four runs that are quick, nimble, and mercurial,
his fingers seemingly inspired by Calliope herself. On Loser, Garcia's
voice is as dust-blown and parched as the tale, barely croaking out some
of the lines. His first solo run underwhelms, but he finishes strong.

In set two, China Cat Sunflower has swift jamming; listen for Brent's
brief paralleling of Garcia's lines (5:50–). Speedy like a Cumberland
Blues stomp, they climb two different peaks before motoring into I
Know You Rider. Garcia squeezes out some soaring fills during Weir's
"backdoor" verse and delivers his own "headlight" line with verve.

On Samson & Delilah, Brent's church-flavored organ elicits visions of
Ray Charles. Around the four-minute mark, it sounds like Garcia wants
to keep soloing, but Weir comes charging in with his "lion's back" verse.
Some great drumming on the final break.

They pick up the pace with Eyes Of The World, a fast version with nearly two minutes of intro. In the final minute, the notes run like frightened mice, Garcia determined to come up with some melodic cheese.

Six songs in, he's still not ready to exit stage left. Who knows how far down this rabbit hole we'll go? After a couple of minutes, we hear sounds that are Lost Sailor-like and then Dark Starish spacey. Then we get something brand new. Still boldly going.

Only two votes from Deadbase respondents in '97 (10/12/84 and 10/31/84 are their top two for the month), a sleeper that should get more attention.

Link to recordings

## 1988 MIAMI, FL
## MIAMI ARENA

After two weeks off, they venture back to the East Coast, playing in this city for the first time in ten years.

Touch Of Grey and Minglewood open; there is plenty of energy here, perhaps energized by thousands of Floridians starved of Grateful Dead since 1985.

Late in the first set, Bird Song builds to an initial peak, then Garcia repeats the main theme (shortened by a note) and drags his still-jamming bandmates back to the vocal.

The closing Promised Land has the energy of the opener. Weir forgets a few lyrics right before he wakes up over Albuquerque. Brent's solo is great (try the soundboard), and the final break is a good rouser.

Set two: China Cat → Rider opens, a peppy pace. I Know You Rider is a bit ordinary until Weir starts singing about the sun. He ups the ante on the second line, Bill and Mickey throw their weight behind it, Lesh gives it a blast and the crowd goes wild. There are more vocal fireworks as Garcia delivers his "headlight" verse.

Next is Saint Of Circumstance, their first in a year (they won't touch it again for six months). A short jam, no passionate rave-up from Garcia. He's Gone has a short exit jam with chords like Bird Song, but they choose not to develop it. Space leads to Goin' Down The Road, some lively locomotion with a melodic Bid You Goodnight-style coda, two runs.

They stay in the key of E, Weir getting a chance to drive his own rocker, I Need A Miracle. Brent gets a chance to close the concert with Dear Mr. Fantasy and the Hey Jude Finale, though Weir has the lead vocal on the latter.

Link to recordings

## 1989 EAST RUTHERFORD, NJ

# BRENDAN BYRNE ARENA

After a night off (Garcia and Weir appeared on *The Late Show With David Letterman*), they perform their third concert here in four days. On this Saturday night near the Big Apple, they have competition, such as the first game of the World Series.

A welcome Help → Slipknot! → Franklin's finishes set one; it's just their second airing of this trio in four years (10/8/89). It will stay in the repertoire the rest of the way.

They make a smooth entrance in and out of Slipknot! Franklin's Tower has a bit of a Foolish Heart lilt to the start. There are some enchanting, Hornsby-esqe licks from Brent after the "listen to the music play" verse.

Scarlet Begonias occupies the third spot in set two, a standalone version. The heart-of-gold-band-jam is a long one (5:26–); it starts with a change of clothes into MIDIfied tones. Soon we hear Garcia's flute and it sounds like a rainforest soundtrack. Where will they go?

Garcia morphs fuzzy and rowdy for their transition into Truckin'. At the end, there are Smokestack/Spoonful sounds (6:45), but they hang it up to see what else is out there, ballooning into a big, gentle sound collage.

At the end of Space, Garcia sounds the first notes of China Doll and they take their time with a long intro. The inside solo is broad shouldered. The exit has some lovely harpsichord tones from Brent.

One More Saturday Night is next and that's their closer, just two songs post-Drums → Space even though Weir sounds like he still has energy to burn.

Link to recordings

## 1994 NEW YORK CITY, NY
# MADISON SQUARE GARDEN

Their second night of six on this stand, Garcia sounds reborn on the set two Fire On The Mountain, part of a pre-Drums section that runs over an hour.

Set one has a Jack Straw start. Vince joins the opening vocals and sure sounds like Hornsby. Bill and Mickey set a quick pace, but Garcia can't seem to get into a good groove on the jam, mostly fits and spurts. West L.A. Fadeaway has an up-tempo jaunt to it and tinkly blues piano from Vince; Garcia is more fluent here.

But it's set two where the lead guitarist plays like a younger incarnation of his considerable self. Scarlet Begonias opens, and in the heart-of-gold-band-jam he's melodic from the start. They navigate a smooth transition into Fire On The Mountain that runs over two minutes. Lesh is playing a major role in propelling this rendition, wonderful lines underneath.

On the first Fire break, Garcia goes to Corrina-like, pedal-steelish effects, then switches back and he's not done. Around eight minutes into the song, he invents a rising theme and leads them to a peak. They take their time getting back down the hill to the next verse. If this had been the entire Fire it would have been plenty good. But there's more.

The next break continues to have interesting lines from Lesh, but this section is less compelling.

In the final Fire On The Mountain jam (17:25–), Garcia again fiddles with melodic motifs and finds a great one after the nineteen-minute mark. Vince climbs aboard and they ride it hard. It sounds like it could have gone on, but Garcia starts the Scarlet theme and they're out. This is the kind of inspired performance you might not figure on hearing in 1994.

Looks Like Rain has more pedal-steel sounds, shades of 1972. Corrina is decent, the singing seems better on this version. The jam picks up speed after the nine-minute mark, and if you squint you might hear a distant Alligator. The tempo is pushed by Lesh and the drummers. Further along in the jam, there's a similar up-tempo pace, vaguely reminiscent of Cumberland Blues and Goin' Down The Road, but they exit into Drums.

Deadbase respondents ranked this second best of the year, a handful of votes behind 3/30/94, and another handful ahead of 10/1/94. They also ranked the Scarlet → Fire second best all-time (Headyversion voters have this version of the duo as tenth best).

Link to recordings

# OCTOBER 15

1966 Sausalito, CA, The Heliport
   (no setlist, no recording)

1976 Los Angeles, CA, Shrine Auditorium

1977 Dallas, TX, Southern Methodist University (SMU),
   Moody Coliseum

1981 Amsterdam, The Netherlands, The Melkweg, The Old Hall
   (Oude Zaal)

1983 Hartford, CT, Hartford Civic Center

1984 Hartford, CT, Hartford Civic Center

1988 St. Petersburg, FL, Bayfront Center
   (1965–2004) (8,600)

1989 East Rutherford, NJ, Brendan Byrne Arena

1994 New York City, NY, Madison Square Garden

1976 LOS ANGELES, CA

## SHRINE AUDITORIUM

This is the last night of the tour, with no additional performances in 1976 until New Year's Eve. Tonight, they play their first He's Gone in two years.

In set one, the final break in Minglewood Blues has some of Garcia's best soloing in the first frame. On the closing Promised Land, he shines as well, pushing his final solo over the moon.

In set two, the exit jam in He's Gone swings some, but it's not quite rollicking. It could be a good fit for Truckin', but they slow it down and spin their wheels, giving way to Drums. From there, we get The Other One, nearly four minutes of jamming before the Spanish lady appears, several strong ground strokes from Lesh.

A long, wandering jam ensues. Around 8:40, Garcia goes elsewhere, lighting upon an Irish jig of a theme that finds him toggling between two chords. His guitar starts to shriek and they roar back into the main theme.

By the eleven-minute mark, they've taken it down to a simmer. Then Lesh strikes a single chord (11:55) to pull them back onto the road as they head to the lily fields. It's probably their best stuff of the night.

Stick around for the long, pretty transition into Comes A Time. The exit jam, nearly four minutes long, picks up speed in the final minute before moving into Franklin's Tower.

Link to recordings

1977 DALLAS, TX

## SOUTHERN METHODIST UNIVERSITY (SMU), MOODY COLISEUM

Tonight's performance of St. Stephen has Garcia penciling out his Ode To Joy (6:45–) that reaches full flower on 1/22/78. And there's a raging double encore.

St. Stephen's answer to The Answer Man is Not Fade Away. It has a driven, hypnotic first break, but it's not quite the maniacal third eye romp that arises on the 1/7/78 version.

Sugar Magnolia starts off as a rhythm track. Garcia is out for maybe two full minutes, and Weir doesn't begin singing until 2:57. Then they raise the roof. Before launching Sunshine Daydream, Weir goes grateful: "Well, now, thank you very much."

Encore: Truckin' into One More Saturday Night. The first Truckin' rave-up starts around the five-minute mark. Then they deliver another one, sneaky and seductive, seven minutes in.

Link to recordings

1981 AMSTERDAM, THE NETHERLANDS

## THE MELKWEG, THE OLD HALL (OUDE ZAAL)

"Now if you don't speak English, ask somebody who does." –BW

After two concerts in France were cancelled, they borrow some instruments and play this small club. Amidst the garage band feel, they perform their first Spoonful.*

The strange gear doesn't seem to bother them. On the opening Minglewood Blues, Garcia is plenty good. For Beat It On Down The Line, they summon the calendar to drive their intro (fifteen beats).

Brent revives Far From Me, their first in over a year, a decent version with some rust showing on the ending. They close with a high-speed Alabama Getaway—the vocals are a bit rushed—into Promised Land.

In set two, the exit jam in He's Gone runs less than ninety seconds before Weir busts out into Spoonful. After a few minutes, they change it up and are headed who knows where. Garcia makes Other One noises and the drummers follow, but they detour into Drums. A brief Space begins with a Lesh solo. Garcia joins, then Weir gets the bus revved up.

On The Other One, Garcia reels off some exciting, repeating ascending runs after the first verse, some of his best work of the night. After the next verse, they drop off a musical cliff and wander into Wharf Rat. During the final jam, Garcia hits the heights.

They close with two Chuck Berry songs, making it three for the night. Johnny B. Goode is the better of these two, a nice solo from Brent.

Encore: Baby Blue.

Link to recordings

*Spoonful, a Willie Dixon song first recorded by Howlin' Wolf (1960).

## 1983 HARTFORD, CT

# HARTFORD CIVIC CENTER

St. Stephen remains, four days after its reappearance at Madison Square Garden. Crowd. Goes. Wild. It's part of an interesting set-two sequence that includes Playing In The Band, China Doll, and a long Garcia-Weir duet in Space.

Feel Like A Stranger starts set one, Garcia solos his behind off, a "new" tune that has really blossomed. On Dire Wolf, we hear his struggling, craggly voice. Minglewood Blues has a great organ solo from Brent. Later, Big Railroad Blues seems apt for Garcia's full gas tank—he's got enough for eleven runs on his second solo.

Fine work on Let It Grow, listen for Weir's whammying chords on the second jam. He's got a good break on his curveball tonight. Day Job closes the set; it's not a fan favorite, but this version contains some of Garcia's better soloing.

Set two: on China Cat Sunflower, Brent brightens it up and later plays the theme you hear at the peak (5:30–5:35). Garcia contributes frenzied soloing on I Know You Rider.

They fiddle with Playing In The Band notes right after Rider, but pause before launching it. The jam stays in highest gear until Weir's strange lick (9:25), one of many inventive phrases he utters along the way. They start circling the wagons around the twelve-minute mark.

Are they done? Garcia makes some Dark Starish sounds before they yield the floor to Bill and Mickey. Or will they?

We then hear Brent's harpsichord and they keep wandering until settling on China Doll, a wonderful transition. There's a great Garcia solo and a couple of minutes of exit jam before Drums, including a final bit of solo chording from Weir.

After three minutes of Space, there's some sweet picking from Weir, and it becomes a duo with Garcia, as they both amp up the pace and duel. Unique. It has the two-chord propulsion to become a Spanish Jam, including a modulation to a minor chord. After the five-minute mark, still a duet, they decide to go somewhere else (is that some Sage And Spirit around eight minutes?).

Weir starts to hit his harmonics and here comes St. Stephen. The answer to The Answer Man is similar to 10/11/83: another St. Stephen jam, then a bit of an awkward slowdown and a stumbling transition into Throwing Stones.

The Throwing Stones jam is wild and weird—listen to Weir's overdriven chords, wow. He takes the next song, too, closing the concert with One More Saturday Night.

Encore: Brokedown Palace, always welcome. Garcia's voice surprisingly clean, he plays a marvelous little solo.

Respondents ranked this sixth best for the year.

Link to recordings

 1984 HARTFORD, CT
## HARTFORD CIVIC CENTER

Playing In The Band is a set two, multi-deck sandwich on this occasion with a unique filling of The Wheel into Wharf Rat. The first set has some compelling performances as well, especially Bird Song.

The opening Hell In A Bucket sounds slightly sluggish and low tempo, but Sugaree is then delivered at a relatively quick pace. The third break is the charm; Garcia plays a melodic theme before his whirling dervish dance. Impressive. If you didn't think he could still raise the roof in '84, try this. Great.

Bird Song bats fourth, Garcia's melodic and mercurial gears at work. Weir chops away, metallic-sounding chords, interesting. They come to a bit of a pause around 7:15, then rebuild. Listen for Weir after nine minutes, speaking in guitar tongues, wow. This rivals some of the great ones (see March '81).

Playing In The Band turns contemplative around 5:30, ebbing and flowing from there, scaling small peaks and quieting back down. By 10:45, you would not guess they'd be at this for another ten minutes.

In the thirteenth minute, it becomes more Space than Jam; Garcia picks out a pretty interstellar pattern (15:00–). Briefly grungy later (18:00–), we get a blast of bass from Lesh. After twenty-one minutes, Bill and Mickey take over.

Five minutes of Drums, then Space which is mostly the two guitars, then just Garcia. He finishes with a delightful little climb into The Wheel.

Wharf Rat's final break starts with a flurry of rustling chords from Garcia and presto! He takes the band back to finish Playing In The Band.

A sleeper of the vintage that would earn more views with an upgraded recording.

Link to recordings

1988 ST. PETERSBURG, FL
## BAYFRONT CENTER

One More Saturday Night opens set two, and what follows is all old-school, 1976 and earlier. But the set feels short. After the opener, we get twenty minutes of songs then Drums.

Set one begins with The Music Never Stopped. On the inside jam, Brent makes some creative sounds, but there's no turn and no three-chord finale. They just move on to Sugaree. But Garcia turns up the heat there after the "cool fool" verse, a great solo.

Brent's new song, Blow Away (#5), is third, complete with his rap after a brief pause mid-song ("take that fist, and hold it up in the air").

Set two: Crazy Fingers is the youngest song in the bunch. Post-Space, they don't veer far from an E blues key and deliver Truckin', Smokestack Lightning, Stella Blue, and Lovelight.

This is a good example of what sounds like an average night for them.

Link to recordings

1989 EAST RUTHERFORD, NJ
## BRENDAN BYRNE ARENA

Just an average performance for this year, with no hint of the magic to come tomorrow night.

Set one opens with the always comfortable Let The Good Times Roll. Brent takes the first verse, Weir the second, Garcia the third. Iko Iko is next; Brent's two organ solos shine, while Garcia's MIDI solo gives the song a Cajun squeeze-box feel.

Victim Or The Crime comes near the end of the set. Weir sounds better on this rendition than others, perhaps because it's more sung than spoken. Garcia plays feverishly during most of the jam.

They close the set with Standing On The Moon (#11). A seemingly strange position for a somber anthem, it would appear just once more in the first frame (3/21/90).

Set two there's a strange start to Samson & Delilah. The drumming kind of breaks down and there's a bit of a restart, Weir leading that effort with his distorted chords. Garcia seems to have it down, but Bill and Mickey have trouble finding the handle.

On Estimated Prophet, Garcia goes to the MIDI early on the inside break, sort of saxy, a bit cartoonish, though there is a brief, stirring peak before Weir picks up the vocals again. On the exit jam, we get Garcia's toothy, MIDI flute, then his marimba/xylophone. On Eyes Of The World, the final minute of the last jam is Garcia & Drums.

Link to recordings

## 1994 NEW YORK CITY, NY
# MADISON SQUARE GARDEN

Their third straight night here before a day off.

Shakedown Street opens, you'll notice Garcia's spunky singing on the chorus. Vince carries most of the jam with piano, synth, and then organ in the final four minutes, all riding on top of Lesh's propulsive bass. They return to the vocals just after the thirteen-minute mark.

Stagger Lee has two long instrumental breaks; check out the solo on the second one, Garcia flashing some melodic lines. Not your typical version.

Candyman is pretty good. There are bits of pretty piano from Vince (you might wish he had more room here), and there's another decent Garcia solo. Easy Answers is next; note the faux horn section.

Set two: Victim Or The Crime has a stretched-out intro, hinting at possibilities. It's nearly a minute before they get to the notes of the main theme. Garcia's guitar utters a stutter in the main jam (7:19–), showing there's still fire in the furnace.

Victim ends with piano notes, a nice segue into Vince's Way To Go Home, a dead ringer for a Steve Winwood tune. It's also a good jam for Garcia with its "I'm A Road Runner" pattern. Vince's singing is loose and free ("any which way").

On New Speedway Boogie, on the penultimate sung chorus, Garcia sings "this darkness got to give" as low down to the ground as you can get (7:27– and 7:43–). Standing On The Moon has a four-minute exit, an expressive solo there. At the very end, it sure sounds like Weir is playing Throwing Stones chords, but Garcia picks his One More Saturday Night lick and that's where they go.

Encore: I Want To Tell You (#5 of seven).

Link to recordings

# OCTOBER 16

1966 San Francisco, CA, Golden Gate Park
(no setlist, no recording)

1970 Philadelphia, PA, University of Pennsylvania,
Irvine Auditorium (setlist, no recording)

1974 San Francisco, CA, Winterland Ballroom

1977 Baton Rouge, LA, Louisiana State University (LSU),
Assembly Center

1981 Amsterdam, The Netherlands, The Melkweg

1988 St. Petersburg, FL, Bayfront Center

1989 East Rutherford, NJ, Brendan Byrne Arena

1974 SAN FRANCISCO, CA

## WINTERLAND BALLROOM

Their first performance in a month is the start of a five-night stand. These will be their final concerts before taking an indefinite break from touring.

A highlight is the thirty-one-minute Playing In The Band. It features sustained improvisation that does not detour long into space or hard dissonance.

The first set shows some rust. During the inside break on Scarlet Begonias, Garcia is amidst his second run when Donna and Weir break into the "wind in the willows" verse. He plows ahead, soloing over their second sung line. He finishes the run, and they sing the lines again.

The set closes with Playing In The Band. Around eleven minutes in, we get a flurry of high bass notes, and soon they catch their first breath. Several minutes later, Lesh sounds some long, large notes, and it becomes more like Space, but quick on its heels they begin a new jam.

Seventeen minutes in, we hear an avant-garde version of trading fours; they toss separate phrases at each other like sonic snowballs before racing off again. It eventually slows (20:35), Garcia plays underwatery tones, Bill's cymbals swish and swirl. Around 22:30, you hear hints of the main Playin' theme. Are they done?

Nope. Lesh starts them down a new road with two notes (24:45) and they build to another peak around the twenty-eight-minute mark, on the wings of a deconstruction of the main theme.

Then they head home.

After Phil & Ned's intermission, there's about twenty-six minutes of what might qualify as Space and then a Jam, none of it particularly compelling. By the twenty-two-minute mark, it becomes Lesh & Drums, then devolves into near silence. Garcia rejoins to start Wharf Rat. It begins with a Dark Star cadence (try singing the latter's lyrics to yourself against this musical intro).

A unique version, they are just a minute or two into the exit jam when they get quiet and jam themselves right out of the song. It becomes a Garcia soliloquy, no drumming, just the lead guitar's lonely notes wandering through the hall. The pretty, quiet exploration continues for another five minutes, until Garcia begins to chord Eyes Of The World.

Encore: Before launching U.S. Blues, Bill Graham asks the crowd to sing Happy Birthday to "Mr. Robert Weir," and they do.

Link to recordings

## 1977 BATON ROUGE, LA
# LOUISIANA STATE UNIVERSITY (LSU) ASSEMBLY CENTER

From SMU to LSU in a day (426 miles). Most of the fireworks are in set one. There are only three songs pre-Drums, but they finish the concert with a flourish.

On Sugaree, Garcia unloads his entire bag of tricks in the first solo, momentous, one of his best efforts. Minglewood Blues is a shining star in the repertoire at this juncture, all the musical parts in sync. The sound has a dangerous edge to it, like a hungry wolf, and Weir is believable as the professional wife-stealer.

The Music Never Stopped closes the set. On the inside jam, Garcia plays a nifty series of descending phrases, then shoots out of there like a rocket. A thrilling finish, at least six runs of his patent-pending trilled chords.

In set two, the more compelling music comes deep in the set. They stretch out the Black Peter "run and see" exit, and by twelve minutes it sounds like the rest of the guys are done with it, but Garcia keeps drilling for oil.

Sure enough, he finds a gusher around the thirteen-minute mark, finishing with an exciting jackhammer pattern that he drives straight into Around And Around. What follows is a great rendition of one of Chuck's classics. They rock the house.

Headyversion voters have Sugaree eighth best all-time, and Black Peter in the top 15 (they also rate Music Never Stopped highly). Weir's 30th birthday.

Link to recordings

## 1981 AMSTERDAM, THE NETHERLANDS
# THE MELKWEG

A special night, their first Turn On Your Lovelight since Pigpen last sang it (5/24/72). They also try Gloria for the second time ever (1/30/68), and debut their first (and only) Hully Gully.* And if that's not enough, set one is all acoustic, shades of Fall 1980.

Start with set two, most of it is a Playing In The Band sandwich with six songs in the middle (no Drums and no Space). The first transition is from Playin' into Hully Gully, then into The Wheel. After moving on to a propulsive Samson & Delilah, they pause for a minute before launching three straight covers, beginning with G-L-O-R-I-A.

It's a great vehicle for Weir's voice, but they won't try it again for three years (11/3/84). In the final minute, they begin an unrelated jam, then the birthday boy gets his third in a row as they turn on Lovelight. It's a great moment in the band's musical history, as most fans dared not dream of hearing this historic closer once exclusively emceed by Pigpen.

After racing through Goin' Down The Road Feelin' Bad, Garcia picks up the Playin' theme. A minute or so of jamming ensues until they finish the song's vocals, bringing the set full circle.

They finish with Black Peter and a rousing Sugar Magnolia with especially energetic guitar from Garcia. No encore.

Deadbase respondents rated this best for the year, likely heavily influenced by the special song list. Other '81 gigs arguably offer better all-around electric set performances, played on their own instruments (e.g., 3/28/81).

Link to recordings

*Hully Gully (1959) The Olympics.

## 1988 ST. PETERSBURG, FL
# BAYFRONT CENTER

Their second night here and there's not much from the birthday boy. Weir leads just two songs in the first frame, and he sings none of the set openers or closers.

The evening's program sounds heavy on the slower stuff and few songs are stretched out. Most of the energy comes at the top of set one. There is some fine soloing from Garcia on the Mississippi Half Step exit (and some kind of violin tones near the "Rio Grandio" chorus).

Brent gets the second song slot, leading them through his bluesy Good Times (Never Trust A Woman). Garcia is good on this one, too, especially his second solo, but the recordings don't capture it well. The song seems to end with Brent's "I feel like hell," but after a pause they finish it off, then jump into Feel Like A Stranger.

Set two: pre-Drums has two rain songs, and a short version of Victim Or The Crime, barely five minutes. Later, Gimme Some Lovin' has the energy you would expect, with Brent's ringing organ and the urgent lead vocals where he's teamed with Lesh.

Perhaps they wanted to save it for the end, closing with All Along The Watchtower and Morning Dew. Garcia turns up the heat on the "young man moan" verse, but the final break remains in low gear, no rave-up.

Encore: Mighty Quinn, preceded by a brief instrumental bow to Weir's 41st birthday.

Link to recordings

## 1989 EAST RUTHERFORD, NJ
# BRENDAN BYRNE ARENA

Another Dark Star tonight, just a week after its revival at Hampton (10/9/89). This one is split into a sandwich that layers Playing In The Band, Uncle John's Band, Drums → Space, I Will Take You Home, and I Need A Miracle.

They don't stop there, keeping the seamless set two going with Attics of My Life and then closing the concert with the back end of Playing In The Band.

Dark Star is a great way to open set two; they deliver a lengthy jam before the first verse (5:37). After ten minutes, it begins to go wiggy and dissonant, but there is light at the end of the tunnel. The first notes of Playing In The Band make for a joyful transition.

The Playin' jam begins with some wonderful high bass notes, then some MIDI flute from Garcia, and organ from Brent. After Uncle John's Band, they pivot back to the Playing In The Band theme. At this point in the set, you'd expect a return to the vocals to finish it, or perhaps a ballad, but they make like a jazz band and explore.

Early in this additional Playin' jam, Garcia turns on the jets and they go full bore into something that is more Space than Drums. But after six minutes, they create a brand-new jam, and briefly touch the Playin' theme again (7:35–). A minute later, we get a great segment led by Brent. Very fresh and inventive jamming.

Deadbase respondents rank this second best on the year, not too far behind 10/9/89.

Link to recordings

# OCTOBER 17

1970 Cleveland, OH, Cleveland Music Hall

1972 St. Louis, MO, Fox Theater

1974 San Francisco, CA, Winterland Ballroom

1978 San Francisco, CA, Winterland Ballroom

1981 Paris, France, Hippodrome de Vincennes

1982 Santa Fe, NM, The Downs at Santa Fe

1983 Lake Placid, NY, Olympic Center Ice Rink

1984 East Rutherford, NJ, Brendan Byrne Arena

1990 Essen, Germany, Grugahalle

1994 New York City, NY, Madison Square Garden

## CLEVELAND MUSIC HALL

This is their first visit to this Cuyahoga River city.

In the early part of the Hard To Handle jam, they almost touch the extra chord that you hear so famously expressed on the 4/29/71 version (B-A-D-F#). Lesh carries it briefly in his bass line.

On Good Lovin' they come out of the Drums section charging hard (8:41). A few minutes later there's a quieter section of trading fours, then it's all Lesh by his lonesome for a bit (12:00–). Before returning to the vocals, we hear an extended section where they play with the Good Lovin' theme in short spurts.

Dark Star runs nineteen minutes but the first verse is missing. After three minutes, we get a long section of near silence, and they don't really begin to come out of that until the eleven-minute mark. Garcia plays one of the key sub-themes in a more relaxed manner (13:20–).

St. Stephen has a raucous rave-up after the "one man gathers" verse (Weir!)—not to be missed. The answer to The Answer Man is Not Fade Away, then a smooth segue into Goin' Down The Road Feelin' Bad (#3). They tack on the Bid You Goodnight coda, then return to Not Fade Away for another sung chorus and the "fade away" refrain before racing into Turn On Your Lovelight. A great finish.

There's more worth exploring here, e.g., That's It For The Other One.

Link to recordings

1972 ST. LOUIS, MO

## FOX THEATER

The first of three nights here, a twenty-three-minute Playing In The Band stands out. It features a jam that never quits, urgent and driven even fourteen minutes in.

Set one also includes a good Black Throated Wind. The exit jam features Weir's impassioned vocals and Garcia's stirring ascending runs.

During China Cat Sunflower, at the turn ending the short inside break, Lesh blasts five big notes and then goes silent, perhaps simply to admire the sound as his tones sail over the audience like sonic soap bubbles (2:16–2:26).

After the three-chord peak (C-G-D) and Weir's nifty little lick, the jam does not go gently into I Know You Rider. Weir starts a punchy chord pattern (5:38–), then Garcia works up his own head of steam. After the "wild geese" verse in Rider, Lesh delivers another noticeable blast of bass, and it seems to stir up Bill as he begins to bash.

Black Peter is one of just five this year. Lesh joins the vocals for the "shine through my window" segment.

Goin' Down The Road has a very different Garcia intro, more blues than country-gospel. Around 1:30 he starts the traditional entry. Stick around for the final solo break, Keith comes to the fore on the third run and takes the cake on the fifth. He also plays some grand, percussive lines during the singing of the final chorus.

Link to recordings

## 1974 SAN FRANCISCO, CA
# WINTERLAND BALLROOM

"…be yourselves, we're all going to be part of an X-rated movie, if all goes well, without any further ado, The Grateful Dead." –BG

Set two offers a seamless sonorous safari beginning with He's Gone. The tail end of the outro jam wanders into a slow shuffle, but Lesh grabs it by the throat and they seem headed into The Other One. Four minutes in, the jamming turns jazzy, bypassing the Spanish lady and detouring into what sounds more like Dave Brubeck than Bolero (and at times like a Playin' jam). After seven minutes, they go further, heading out into the quiet vacuum of uncharted musical space.

There's atonal angst ahead; buckle up. By fourteen minutes, it's near silence, occasionally punctuated by a twist on Garcia's volume knob or an electric piano keystroke. Then suddenly Lesh springs to life (15:29) and the bus rolls again.

The Spanish lady makes a very late entrance (18:01–). After several minutes, they pivot into Spanish Jam. Keith, Weir, Lesh, and Kreutzmann lead the start of it, Garcia joins later on slide. It's a short one, with Garcia taking them into the descending pattern suggesting a Mind Left Body Jam (it has a middle part between the descending segments).

Lesh then steers them back to finish The Other One, including a mini rave-up and verse two, before winding down into Stella Blue. Beautifully sung, Keith's grand piano and Garcia's guitar lines on the exit are birds in flight, ending far too soon. Quite a journey.

There's more to the set than meets the ear, such as the last couple of minutes of the Scarlet Begonias jam, and the classic bounce of Big River.

The set one China Cat Sunflower has an extended jam that includes the "Feelin' Groovy" segment, three runs worth. They close that set with Weather Report Suite; they'll do that piece just once more (tomorrow night) before carrying on with Let It Grow as a standalone song (6/3/76).

Double encore: Casey Jones, and U.S. Blues for the second straight night.

Deadbase respondents in '97 gave this performance just three votes, far behind the final three nights.

Link to recordings

## 1978 SAN FRANCISCO, CA
# WINTERLAND BALLROOM

"Anybody out there from New York? You might like to know, that the Yankees won the Series…" –PL

This is their first performance in a month, the start of five nights here. A couple of the new songs get a workout during the first half, I Need A Miracle (#5) and Stagger Lee (#4). Jack Straw closes the set, Garcia goes to his chords early (ninth run) and sticks with them to the end.

Set two: they open with what will soon become a regular pre-Drums foursome: Scarlet → Fire, Estimated → Eyes. The opening Scarlet has a lengthy vocal flub, but there are none in Fire.

Eyes Of The World has an extended intro, Garcia invents some interesting phrases (1:37–) and builds to a small peak. He shows bursts of speed in places during the first break, and Weir later makes some interesting contributions (5:45–). Another phrase from Garcia blooms (6:30–), then they knit and purl quietly to themselves.

In Drums, after ten minutes, the skins yield to bells and chimes, then Garcia joins. Later, Weir layers on some light slide. After Lesh enters, it resembles Space, the perfect musical milieu for If I Had The World To Give.

Just their second performance of this song, the exit jam is built upon a unique chord progression (A flat to C), a canvas clearly to Garcia's liking. He takes fifteen runs, stuttering on the twelfth and keeping that up through the rest.

They close with Around And Around. There's a rough beginning to the main break (Garcia drops out, or perhaps it's a technical glitch), but what a finish, slick speed and wonderful rock 'n' roll licks.

Link to recordings


## 1981 PARIS, FRANCE

# HIPPODROME DE VINCENNES

After two nights in Amsterdam, they make their first visit to France since 1974. Reunited with their own instruments, we get a unique set two opener: Truckin' → Bird Song → Never Trust A Woman.

Truckin' begins with a drum major's whistle and a snippet of parade music. The exit jam has some call and response between Garcia and Brent, then a quick wind down and smooth transit into Bird Song. That jam slows some around 6:30, then Garcia starts picking at what's left. Rather than returning to the vocals, they float and tiptoe their way into Brent's blues.

On Estimated Prophet, during the inside break Brent steps up, blasting away on his organ (4:53–) before returning to Weir's vocals. During a mostly plodding exit jam, Bill and Mickey kick up the pace around the ten-minute mark and Garcia starts running. It gets interesting from there.

Eyes Of The World features some good jamming, Garcia starts the first break with a creative opening lick (2:08). On the second break, there's a bend that soars the skies (4:43), then we get another skyscraper after he switches to chords (5:31). It's a bit disjointed, but he's clearly in the mood to push the envelope rather than just noodle.

Morning Dew is their sixth of seven this year. The final jam goes church quiet, and they take their time before the rebuild. Garcia then dazzles as he pulls out his trilled chords (twice!). He's barely finished singing "anyway-ay-ay" before playing the opening lick to Around And Around. Weir takes the second verse down to a near whisper, then goes hyper-sonic on the rest. He gets the next song, too, closing with One More Saturday Night.

It's a well-played, spirited performance, worth a full listen, with interesting notes from Garcia throughout.

Link to recordings

## 1982 SANTA FE, NM

## THE DOWNS AT SANTA FE

They visit The Land of Enchantment for the first time in five years. Just one performance here, then a six-week break.

Set two: Estimated Prophet gets off to a strange start, as Weir's guitar seems to vanish thirty seconds in. When he returns, they do the "California" chorus, words and all. He then goes back to verse one to begin the tune properly. Then he skips verse two, going straight to the "you would not believe me" bridge.

On He's Gone, they end the usual jam quickly (8:25) and then begin a couple of brand-new improvisations before Drums, each worthy of further development.

After Space, we get Throwing Stones (#9). The song ends with a short, acapella "ashes ashes, all fall down," then just a tad of jamming before Garcia starts Goin' Down The Road Feelin' Bad.

They mostly skip that song's traditional ending coda, feeling their way into The Wheel, the only time they tried this transition. The Other One is next; the jam between verses has a stirring bit of chord play from Weir near the end (4:20–4:30). From "comin' around" they are into Wharf Rat in ten seconds.

Link to recordings

## 1983 LAKE PLACID, NY
# OLYMPIC CENTER ICE RINK

This is a good example of a performance in which the first set is more compelling than the second.

An epic Sugaree opens. Over sixteen minutes long, with three full solos, it is certainly one of the longest. Garcia's first solo is nothing special, but his second has a good peak (7:30–) and then an exciting frenzied rush (7:40–). During the third, he goes into whirling dervish mode early (10:55–) and generally plays like the Tasmanian Devil until switching to chords around 13:55. Bill and Mickey then start bashing and they return to the vocals.

Later in the set, Bird Song features boisterous runs during the jam. They follow with two strong set-closing tunes. On Hell In A Bucket, Garcia's guitar briefly rings like an alarm bell (4:05), then he hits a particularly quirky high note (4:11). Weir's enthusiasm bubbles over: "Least I'm enjoyin' the ride, like a friend of mine used to say, ride Sally ride!"

During Deal, the exit jam almost calms for a moment around the five-minute mark, but a brilliant peak is just around the corner, the band hitting on all cylinders. Garcia is still going gangbusters seven minutes in. There's simply no quit in him as he finds a new guitar figure and rides it like a bucking bronco (7:30–). The jam finally calms down around 8:30.

Set two: To Lay Me Down is their first in a year, and Garcia surprisingly has the voice for it. Played just three times in 1982, they won't touch it again for five years (3/27/88). The pretty solo shows the song is a close cousin of Brokedown Palace.

Post-Space, The Wheel's exit jam shifts gears around 5:30 and we get an exploratory jam. There's never really been a Weir ballad tailor-made for the late set two slot, so we get a major change of mood with I Need A Miracle. Garcia is on fire during the inside solo, and he powers ahead on the exit jam before Weir is done singing the refrain.

Goin' Down The Road gives Garcia another road to rampage; it starts at a moderate tempo (listen to Weir's cool harmonics at the start).

They close with Good Lovin' for three rockers in a row.

"I don't have to tell you what it's like these days…sometimes you can't see sh-t through the smoke and the haze…push back the night…up to me and you…" –BW

Encore: Revolution (#2).

Just outside the Deadbase respondents' top ten for the year (Heady-version voters have this Sugaree third all-time, ahead of 5/19/77 by a handful of votes).

Link to recordings

## 1984 EAST RUTHERFORD, NJ
# BRENDAN BYRNE ARENA

The first of two here, not a particularly crisp performance.

They open with Iko Iko, and Garcia starts by dropping the lead vocal. When he comes back, you'll notice the rough, scraggly voice quality, but there's still that guitar and his ability to improvise endlessly on this tune. Promised Land has a great organ solo from Brent, but they seem to fumble the ending.

Set two is better, they handle the opening Help → Slipknot! → Franklin's fairly well. Slipknot! runs over eight minutes, Garcia romps through most of it like a charging rhino until a slight intermission around 6:30.

On Truckin' the exit jam quickly morphs into a slow blues (6:20–), but it's not Nobody's Fault (contrary to listings in Deadbase and other sources) (no recording has a separate track for it). It sounds closer to Spoonful, but it's over in less than a minute when Garcia picks out Stella Blue.

At the end of Stella Blue, on the heels of Garcia's tornado twirl (check out Brent aping those licks), he launches Goin' Down The Road. The ending is really mucked up, as Garcia abandons the traditional coda for god knows what.

Encore: Brokedown Palace. You'll need to whistle through your teeth and spit when Garcia muffs the last two lines of verse two. A far gone lullaby, indeed.

Deadbase respondents rated half a dozen other October '84 concerts higher.

Link to recordings

## 1990 ESSEN, GERMANY
# GRUGAHALLE

After three days off and over eight hundred miles south, they begin their mini tour of Germany. It's kind of a Weir-dominated night, as he gets six of the nine lead vocals in set one, including the opener and the closer.

They have plenty of energy on the opening Hell In A Bucket. Sugaree is next; Hornsby has the final solo, then Garcia comes charging hard on his heels with a flurry of trilled chords (6:05–), a great segment.

Mid-set, Me & My Uncle into Maggie's Farm, Vince is in the background with a violin sound on both. It's their first Maggie's Farm in three years (11/14/87), the lead vocals are shared: Weir, Garcia, Hornsby, Vince, then Lesh. The crowd eats it up.

Set two opens with China Cat Sunflower → I Know You Rider. Garcia serves a fine little rave-up on the first Rider break, but the soloing after the "headlight" verse is less lively.

There's not much of an exit jam out of The Wheel. They kind of muddle around before Weir starts I Need A Miracle. Garcia's solo here has some teeth, and on the final break is that Vince honking like a sax player? (4:10–). Garcia's nifty little turn leads them into Black Peter.

Link to recordings


## 1994 NEW YORK CITY, NY

# MADISON SQUARE GARDEN

After a Sunday off, they play their fourth of six here. Of note is the Midnight Hour opener, and the Rainy Day Women encore (with Bob Dylan on stage). It's an older-school kind of evening—only one of their newer originals is played (Eternity).

In The Midnight Hour is a generally rare song selection, performed barely once a year in the '90s (there would be no more after this one). Vince's horn-like synth blasts sound before the ending (4:40).

Peggy-O is next, and Garcia's voice is in fine shape. Minglewood Blues starts with Weir's hyper distorted, grungy sound, and then a variety of keyboard tones from Vince including horn. The song is far from its days as a raging beast.

The Eternity jam rises to a dissonant peak, they come out of it after the six-minute mark. Weir picks up the vocals again at eight minutes ("love won't, ever die"). On Friend Of The Devil, Vince gets a piano solo, two runs.

Set two: Eyes Of The World opens, they arrange a long, atmospheric introduction with more Vince than Garcia. The first verse comes around the six-minute mark, you may notice the different vocal accents ("nut *thatch* winter's...wings a *mile* long"). On the first break, Garcia is in higher gear.

Verse two (the redeemer) comes at 12:30, Vince is more prominent on this break; there's a flash of speed (15:44) and then it's Garcia's turn. The song is sort of huffing and puffing by 18:45, but Garcia seems up for more. He starts some clever chord play (21:40), the drummers begin to muscle up, and we get the third verse.

It winds down for two minutes, and suddenly you realize the set just started and won't be yielding to Drums. Instead, Weir tees up Women Are Smarter.

After Drums → Space (over thirty minutes long), they close with All Along The Watchtower and Morning Dew. There's a fairly long wind down between the two, some stray piano and guitar notes. Their seventh Morning Dew of eight this year, Garcia's voice is still strong late in the set, and he brings his trilled chords (10:59) for one run.

Encore: Rainy Day Women #12 and #35 (#3). Bob Dylan joins—you can hear him at the start of the lead vocals. This is their first rendition in seven years (7/26/87), and it turned out to be their last.

A decent Fall '94 performance, worth a full listen. Deadbase respondents in 1997 ranked this fourth best on the year, just ahead of 10/1/94 and 10/5/94.

Link to recordings

# OCTOBER 18

1968 Torrance, CA, The Bank
   (no setlist, no recording)

1970 Minneapolis, MN, Tyrone Guthrie Theatre
   (partial setlist, no recording)

1972 St. Louis, MO, Fox Theater

1974 San Francisco, CA, Winterland Ballroom

1978 San Francisco, CA, Winterland Ballroom

1980 New Orleans, LA, Saenger Theatre

1983 Portland, ME, Cumberland County Civic Center

1984 East Rutherford, NJ, Brendan Byrne Arena

1988 New Orleans, LA, University of New Orleans,
   Kiefer Lakefront Arena

1989 Philadelphia, PA, The Spectrum

1994 New York City, NY, Madison Square Garden

1972 ST. LOUIS, MO

## FOX THEATER

A big set two, starting with a Playing In The Band sandwich (their first!) that wraps a twenty-eight-minute Dark Star and Morning Dew.

A fine Playin' jam, the three-guitar weave is in all its early glory, riding on top of some great drumming. Consistent percolation, Bill stokes the fire around 11:50 and it boils over a minute later.

Never turning bitter or dissonant, they quiet in the final minute until Bill has the stage to himself. An early slot for a drum solo, it's short-lived, and out of the blue comes Lesh with the Dark Star melody.

Six minutes in, they lower down and wander softly, until Lesh once again sounds the main theme (9:57–). It then builds to a peak, and we get the first verse (11:38). Some wonderfully inventive and weird improvisation thereafter. By nineteen minutes, they've descended to the bottom of their atonal abyss.

This is where we get several blasts of Wagnerian bass from Lesh. He solos and eventually begins a brand-new song (22:53–) accompanied by Bill. More than one commentator has referred to this as the "Philo Stomp."*

Several minutes later, another motif arises out of the blue, as Lesh starts up the four-note "Feelin' Groovy" theme. From there, they move seamlessly into Morning Dew, bypassing the second Dark Star verse.

During the final break of Morning Dew, Garcia brings his buzzsaw (10:37–), but instead of finishing with a vocal line, they seem to abruptly drop back into a Playin' jam.

Link to recordings

*For the "Philo Stomp" see, e.g., 10/24/72; 10/28/72; and 11/13/72.

## 1974 SAN FRANCISCO, CA
## WINTERLAND BALLROOM

This is the third of five concerts on this stand. It becomes a three-set performance as the Ned & Phil intermezzo leads to a lengthy Jam, Dark Star, Morning Dew, and then a break. Promised Land begins a final frame of seven songs (plus the encore).

Dark Star has a beautiful, longish introduction with a fake entrance. Garcia sounds the main theme as if he's ready to begin verse one (5:55–) then twitters and flies off. In his further wandering, he finds and repeats a lovely five-note motif before beginning the vocal.

Later, there's a wonderful series of seven or so runs, each one punctuated by Garcia hitting a distinctive low note (11:55–). Approaching the fifteen-minute mark, they create something completely new. The drums and piano are prominent, it begins with a mood like Weather Report Suite: Prelude, then gets slightly funky and syncopated similar to early '70s R&B (e.g., Bill Withers' "Use Me").

After a few minutes, it devolves into drumming and spacey sounds. Like two years ago to the day, they again forego verse two of Dark Star and walk out into a Morning Dew (their eleventh and final coupling of these two songs).

This is a profound performance of Morning Dew. A rich sound, featuring prodigious bass and truly grand piano. Delicate and dynamite. It may bring tears.

The best band in the land.

Deadbase respondents ranked this concert among the top five for the year (they voted Morning Dew third best version all-time; it was ranked fourth among Headyversion voters).

Link to recordings

## 1978 SAN FRANCISCO, CA

# WINTERLAND BALLROOM

This is the second of five on this run. A mix of newer tunes, rousing lead guitar, flubbed vocals (Terrapin Station), and a unique Mind Left Body Jam out of Drums.

The new songs continue to get a workout—it's the second straight night for Stagger Lee (#5) and I Need A Miracle (#6), along with the second performance of Donna's From The Heart Of Me.

Sugaree opens, the tempo is a bit overcooked, and there's not much of note in the first two breaks. But your patience will be somewhat rewarded, as deep into the third break Garcia begins to invent dreamy phrases, finding a beauty—one note followed by five, repeating—he crowns with a silky soaring bend.

On Stagger Lee, Garcia's singing is clear, three runs on his solo. After the final vocal, he throws down some big power chords that almost drown out Weir's slide licks.

The closing Music Never Stopped has a hair-raising end to the inside jam, Garcia shrieking at the high end of his fretboard. The closing jam features his wobbly, then trilled chords, six full runs.

In set two, there are seven songs pre-Drums, just two after. A crisp Samson & Delilah is fifth in this frame. Terrapin Station bats sixth, and perhaps Garcia is tiring. He bungles one verse ("eyes alight") and can't seem to find the next one ("which of you to gain me tell"), forcing a merciful dive into what becomes a much longer than usual inside solo passage. He skips over the first "sailor" verse, sings the next one, then launches another solo.

The rest of it goes far better, sung with conviction, plus a particularly scintillating line leaping out of Garcia's guitar during the outro (11:10).

Playing In The Band is relatively subdued, quieting by 5:30 into light hand drumming, lead guitar noodling, and occasional bass notes. Keith and Weir seem to disappear, and it becomes purely a Garcia and Drums affair for the final three (interesting) minutes.

After five minutes of Drums, Bill and Mickey are joined by Lee Oskar, a Danish harmonica player. It starts with a cantina sound, Caribbean drum, and lonesome harp. Garcia joins, and it eventually picks up the "got my mojo workin'" theme. Weir alters this when he layers on the four descending chords to the Mind Left Body Jam (2:47–). There's an initial four runs of that before Weir returns to the "mojo" theme, then they toggle back and forth between the two.

Truckin' closes the show, Weir sings confidently ("more or less in line, we just keep truckin' on—well traveled"). The initial build is low key for this song, but they are far from done. Garcia brandishes his chords then leads them, raging, into another build after the eight-minute mark, this one more of a rocket ship. Lesh blasts away after the peak. Now what?

There wasn't much of a roadmap for closing a concert with Truckin' (see, e.g., 1/6/78). They go through a third build, this one a unique variation, until they just try to stomp the life out of the fire-breathing dragon.

Encore: I Need A Miracle (#6). They wind it all the way down to a sing-along that fades away.

Link to recordings

## 1980 NEW ORLEANS, LA
## SAENGER THEATRE

A four-day break behind them, the band performs in New Orleans for the first time in over ten years. Despite the setting, we get a standard setlist and not much of note musically. As with the Warfield gigs, there are three sets, the first is acoustic.

Set two has some sound issues early in the opening Alabama Getaway. The exit jam is short, a feature of most songs tonight. Brent is a bright spot in many places, such as his solo on Big River (tinkly toy piano, three runs).

Althea starts very low-key, with ultra soft drumming; there's just a short solo after the "space is getting hot" verse. During the "born to be a bachelor" verse, it sounds like the song will run out of gas. The final break is limited to eight lines of soloing wrapped by restatements of the main melody. Don't look for catharsis here.

In the final set, deep into Feel Like A Stranger, Garcia starts to find some new stuff, one of the few inventive moments of interest tonight (7:13–). Ship Of Fools is like Althea, on the sluggish side of slow, with a solo full of tiny, tentative notes.

Space has some intense feedback from Lesh (2:10–), you will feel the vibrations. It becomes an interesting little jam, then dissolves before they launch Not Fade Away.

Black Peter is particularly restrained like the other ballads tonight. The start of Garcia's inside solo nearly begins behind the beat, and most of the rest of it keeps a low profile. The final break is more energetic but short, as if there was a curfew tonight on each of the exits.

The soundboard recording may create a different impression for listeners, but this is not one of the better performances from the Fall '80 tour.

Link to recordings

## 1983 PORTLAND, ME
# CUMBERLAND COUNTY CIVIC CENTER

This is another fine Fall '83 performance, many of the highlights come in the first set.

On the opening Jack Straw, the final break features a rousing conclusion of power chords and Weir's whammy bar (twenty-five runs!). The effervescent energy spills over into the following They Love Each Other, vocals bright.

Dupree's Diamond Blues has more of that same exuberant singing from Garcia. On C.C. Rider, Brent takes the song to a higher level, and it turns into a barnburner. Weir seems to drop out briefly amidst his slide solo (5:05), but it's decent until he voyages beyond the 20th fret. From there, they really dig in and pile drive it, an inspired cutting contest with nobody looking for the exit door.

Althea has expressive singing. The final solo starts with slashing chords, then single notes that range all over the fretboard. We get more chords, then another round of spirited soloing, a boisterous bacchanal.

On Lazy Lightnin' Weir sounds a bit hoarse, and he eases up on some of the lyrics ("rope of fire"). During the Supplication jam, after the two-minute mark, Weir lets fly with whammied lines. It quiets around 3:30, then rebuilds with some strong drones from Brent.

China Cat Sunflower opens set two. The transition jam has shimmering, metallic sound waves in the background that run through I Know You Rider. There are some exciting moments in the jam, as it starts to cook around 5:45, Garcia playing his rear off, driving it to an exciting peak.

By the time they get to Estimated Prophet, Weir's voice has made a complete recovery. You'll hear some classic, full-bore Weirding right at the start of Garcia's solo (7:51–8:23). They take the exit jam down in fifteen seconds for a smooth transition into He's Gone.

Perhaps underrated, nary a vote from Deadbase respondents in '97 (nine other October concerts got votes).

Link to recordings

## 1984 EAST RUTHERFORD, NJ
# BRENDAN BYRNE ARENA

A solid performance here, top to bottom. "This first one's a drummer's choice." –BW

The band opens with Feel Like A Stranger. It's tight from the start, a dancing beat, simmering improvisation. This does not sound like a band on its last legs, or even past its prime.

Then it's a complete change of gears. Candyman, this one a beautiful example of Garcia's command of both vocals and guitar, with many nuanced accents:

* the "I come in from Memphis" line

* the tiny guitar figure he tacks on to "talk the jive"

* the "wager" verse, stretching a word like a rubber band— "lay it on the li-i-i-i-ine"—then biting it off with another quick guitar lick

Weir follows with Little Red Rooster, his own take on life as a ladies' man. After Brent's fine B3 solo, there's no need to hide the women and children as Weir's slide work thankfully avoids a run into the higher register (a rarely used template).

Hell In A Bucket closes set one with great energy (Cf. 10/1/84 re: speed). But there's an oops moment after the "Z-rated scenes" verse and the following chorus. As Weir starts to sing the "you analyze me" bridge, Garcia leaps into a solo. He quickly shuts it down, but seems a bit shaken by the error, and his following solo starts more tentatively. Weir's final vocals receive special echoing effects.

Set two is upbeat and up-tempo with only one ballad. Dancin' In The Streets opens, it's one of the better late-era versions. Garcia's playing is speedy, and he finds a creative phrase or two. The jam sounds like a distant cousin of a Here Comes Sunshine break. Also noticeable are the long drum rolls sprinkled in.

Touch Of Grey is also fast-paced, perhaps too much, as Garcia has a hard time keeping up during his first solo run.

The centerpiece of the set is a Playing In The Band sandwich with four layers. The Playin' jam is contemplative, more simmer than sear. After eight minutes, it takes a spacey turn, then a nifty shift into Uncle John's Band, Garcia inventing a variation of the UJB theme and reverse engineering their way in.

After the final Uncle John's vocal, Garcia plays the Playin' theme (10:50–) and noodles around on it for over a minute, though some setlists don't reflect this.

China Doll is next. Garcia's voice is seriously challenged here (you may wince), but the lovely exit jam soothes the savage breath with pearly, angelic notes, and then...

Away he goes! (5:25–), charging forth like a stallion in the wind, something you might hear in a Let It Grow jam. They ride into Drums, with a wonderfully weird electronic figure from Brent at the end.

After Space, Garcia picks up the Playin' theme and they finish it off. Weir closes the concert with Throwing Stones and Not Fade Away (he sang all the set openers and closers tonight).

Encore: Baby Blue.

A sleeper of the Fall '84 vintage, a handful of votes from respondents in '97.

Link to recordings

## UNIVERSITY OF NEW ORLEANS, KIEFER LAKEFRONT ARENA

After a day off and a long left turn from St. Petersburg, Florida (681 miles), they pull in for one here. There's a double encore and guest appearances by The Neville Brothers and The Bangles.

Start with Drums. It sounds like more hands at work than usual, a multilayered sound thanks to one or more Neville Brothers. They keep banging as the track shifts to Space, Garcia making Other One noises early. You'll notice that there really is no Space here; the first four minutes is much more a prelude to The Other One.

But then, around 4:45, they ditch it, and we get swirling, swooshing sounds, then chimes, and out of this dreamscape comes Brent singing I Will Take You Home.

From there, they pick up the shards of The Other One and seek out the Spanish lady. It's a quick bus ride—they cover both verses in six minutes, and there are heavy effects on Weir's vocals.

Encores: Iko Iko (Art Neville sings and plays keyboard) and Knockin' On Heaven's Door.

Link to recordings

## 1989 PHILADELPHIA, PA
# THE SPECTRUM

The first of three in a row here. Several numbers get more than a full-length treatment: Shakedown Street (over fourteen minutes); Bird Song (thirteen); and Terrapin Station (seventeen). Garcia plays his Wolf equipped with MIDI, and he tries many different settings on various tunes. It's an effects-laden performance.

Set one: don't let the short list fool you, it's nearly an hour of music. Shakedown Street starts, and the new sounds begin amidst the jam (8:35–). On Bird Song, we get MIDI-flute (8:19–9:21) and the usual late-era build.

Set two: on I Know You Rider, the soloing here is more muscular, bolstered by new effects. On Ship Of Fools, the notes sound rounder and slightly less distorted than what we typically hear on, say, Candyman. Women Are Smarter has an odd tone during the first solo. They don't quite stop on a dime in ending that tune, Garcia strums chords for awhile before starting Terrapin Station.

The Terrapin exit jam sounds orchestral, with machine gun effects (11:28–). After the thirteen-minute mark, they leave the Terrapin jam behind and begin a new one, led by Garcia's trumpet soloing. Some brief Dark Starish noodling (16:55–) appears before giving way to Drums.

Deadbase respondents gave this concert two votes, while ranking half a dozen October '89 concerts far higher (their top four of the year: 10/9/89, 10/16/89, 10/8/89, 10/26/89) (Headyversion voters rated Bird Song eleventh best all-time, tied with 3/7/81).

Link to recordings

1994 NEW YORK CITY, NY

## MADISON SQUARE GARDEN

The fifth of six on this stand, they open ambitiously with Help On The Way → Slipknot! → Franklin's Tower.

They handle both ends of Slipknot! well. Franklin's Tower has a long intro where Garcia seems to disappear until a minute and a half in. The first verse comes late (2:53), but he sounds fine. The set has an underwhelming finish with Childhood's End (#6 of eleven) and Don't Ease Me In.

In set two, out of He's Gone they skip an exit jam in favor of something else, as Weir steers them into Smokestack Lightning. Their second rendition this year, a perennial since the 10/9/84 revival. There are some sparkly blues piano runs from Vince here and there. After Truckin', we get a brief "jam" that doesn't do much; the following Drums section has far more drive and ingenuity.

Space—sixteen minutes worth—starts to get dissonant a third of the way in, then shrill (7:09). This one is not a pleasant cruise on a New Age houseboat.

This performance only received two votes from Deadbase respondents, but perhaps the soundboard and/or the video will render the performance more compelling for listeners.

Link to recordings

# OCTOBER 19

1968 Las Vegas, NV, Jaycees Clark County Fair, Convention Center (no setlist, no recording)

1971 Minneapolis, MN, University of Minnesota, Cyrus Northrop Memorial Auditorium

1972 St. Louis, MO, Fox Theater

1973 Oklahoma City, OK, Fairgrounds Arena

1974 San Francisco, CA, Winterland Ballroom

1980 New Orleans, LA, Saenger Theatre

1981 Barcelona, Spain, Sports Palace

1989 Philadelphia, PA, The Spectrum

1990 Berlin, Germany, ICC Berlin

1994 New York City, NY, Madison Square Garden

1971 MINNEAPOLIS, MN

## UNIVERSITY OF MINNESOTA, NORTHROP AUDITORIUM

"They're called The Grateful Dead."

A night filled with firsts:

* Keith Godchaux's first performance

* The first night of the Fall tour

* Their first performance of six songs: Tennessee Jed; Jack Straw; Mexicali Blues; Comes A Time; One More Saturday Night; and Ramble On Rose

The first set has fifteen songs, including five of the new ones. They open with Bertha, which has a rocking tempo and fabulous drumming. Tennessee Jed is taken seriously up-tempo, like the early versions of They Love Each Other. And there's a slight twist on a key lyric ("listen to the whistle of the passin' train"). Two full runs on the lead guitar solo.

On Jack Straw, the first verse is a joint affair, with Weir and Lesh leading the vocals. Weir takes the bridge lyrics by himself; Garcia sticks to his guitar. Keith and Bill are big contributors to the ensemble sound. Listen for the Lesh blast after Weir's "not with all."

For Mexicali Blues, Lesh joins Weir in full throat on the choruses. Comes A Time starts with Garcia strumming chords, a cadence like Brokedown Palace. The "you've got an empty cup" lyric gets a falsetto treatment, and there's an extra verse ("When the words come out, like an angry stream") (see also 10/26/71).

They slot the rookie One More Saturday Night in front of the set one closer Casey Jones, a great rocker from day one.

"OK, for anyone who tuned in late and for all the people here, The Grateful Dead."

Set two: after a Truckin' opener we get the last of the new ones, Ramble On Rose. It's given a faster tempo than what became the standard version and has a couple of slightly different lyrics, e.g., "pace the halls, climb the walls, beat it before they blow" (and "the wine ain't sweeter, on the far side of the hill."). Garcia takes an initial solo after the first verse and chorus, then a second in the traditional setting after the "leader of the band" line.

The main meal is That's It For The Other One, though at this time Cryptical Envelopment is decidedly shorter (the drum solo inside nearly equals the Cryptical bookends).

Link to recordings

## 1972 ST. LOUIS, MO
# FOX THEATER

It's their third straight night here. The Other One features He's Gone in the middle.

In set two Truckin' is in low gear through the verses. The exit jam seems headed into Other One territory in the final minute—you can hear it in Lesh's lines—but they hand it off to Bill before launching it.

This version starts with more of a Lesh solo than his classic rumbling bass line, but then he summons a close cousin. A low-key start to the song ensues more conversation than cacophony. Four minutes later, Garcia latches onto a lick with a Dark Star motif and they ride.

After the Spanish lady verse (5:05–), in less than two minutes, we descend into Space. Garcia focuses on a repeating lick, Keith mimics it, and suddenly they are out of the soup and riding once again. Keith is on electric piano, and with Bill's drumming, it starts to resemble a Chick Corea session. Garcia, Lesh, and Weir then drop out, and for a while it's just those two (9:57–).

The rest of the band drops back in around the eleven-minute mark, chugging along at the pace of a Caution jam. Some fine jamming ensues from there, including some screeching, Alice in Wonderland wobblies from Garcia (13:57–). Weir picks up the main theme (16:20), but rather than sing verse two, they pull on the reins and begin He's Gone.

The exit jam there features a great final minute, morphing from pretty arpeggios to Truckin' rave-ups, then back into The Other One and the lily fields verse.

The concert closes with the Not Fade Away → Goin' Down The Road couplet. There's an odd start to Goin' Down The Road as they don't quite nail the transition from Not Fade Away. Garcia doesn't begin the introductory theme until 1:30, and it's quite subdued. It picks up steam after the five-minute mark once Bill steps on the gas.

Link to recordings

## 1973 OKLAHOMA CITY, OK
# FAIRGROUNDS ARENA

This is the start of the Fall tour and their first gig in over three weeks. The Mind Left Body Jam makes its debut,* and the concert finishes with a triple encore that is nearly long enough to be considered a third set.

Dark Star is the sixth song in set two; they tune up for over a minute before Lesh starts it. A wonderful wander, the first verse is nowhere in sight after six minutes. They finally revisit the theme (13:32), and quickly thereafter Garcia sings the first verse. It's mostly Lesh and Bill after sixteen minutes, then a new jam emerges: Garcia plays briefly on slide, Bill mixes up the rhythm, and Keith plays electric piano. It could be anything.

Garcia picks up the slide again and we eventually begin to get the descending chord pattern that forms the heart of the Mind Left Body Jam. That part has a Dear Prudence flavor to it. There's also a defined bridge between the descending sections.

They finish it quickly and float off into space (4:30–). Garcia becomes a shrieking, hypersonic, wobbling top before they quiet once again into a vast emptiness from which they begin Morning Dew. The inside jam features gargantuan bass blasts from Lesh. In a beautiful start to the exit jam, Garcia briefly quotes some Bach (9:23–).

The first encore is Eyes Of The World and it's a set-worthy rendition, over fourteen minutes in length. Not an afterthought, it ranks among the better ones this year (listen to Garcia's surprising fill after they sing the "wake up to find out" line). Still hard charging in the final minute, they power down in fifteen seconds to begin Stella Blue. They finish with Johnny B. Goode.

Link to recordings

*per Deadbase; see also 3/5/72.

## 1974 SAN FRANCISCO, CA

# WINTERLAND BALLROOM

In the fourth night of five here, they create a unique Sugar Magnolia sandwich wrapping He's Gone, Truckin', Black Peter, and assorted condiments.

Garcia has a fine moment in the Sugar Magnolia jam, a run up the mountain expressing pure joy (5:05–). They make the usual pause for Sunshine Daydream but detour into He's Gone.

During the exit jam, Lesh puts the brakes on, then Garcia steers them into Truckin'. But the "arrows of neon" don't come, and it becomes a jam, soon featuring drumming and a bass line that resembles Caution.

Two minutes in, it sounds like the kind of improvisation you might have heard in Lovelight long ago. They hand it off to Bill for a minute before rejoining what should be called Space; it becomes particularly quiet and pretty around the eight-minute mark. They fall into a Roadhouse Blues kind of vamp (9:45–) before launching Truckin' again.

From there, they go into a blues of another sort—Black Peter—and after a noticeable pause, Sunshine Daydream.

Double encore: One More Saturday Night and U.S. Blues.

The first set treats include their first Mama Tried in three years (7/31/71) (Weir has some trouble with the lyrics), and the eighteen-minute Eyes Of The World.

Link to recordings

## 1980 NEW ORLEANS, LA
## SAENGER THEATRE

Another three-set performance, this one sounds less constrained at times and finishes well.

The acoustic set has some great soloing by Garcia in Bird Song, with two separate peaks. This version runs a couple minutes longer than the Warfield renditions. They also stretch out on Heaven Help The Fool.

The set two opening Jack Straw is a candidate for longest ever—Garcia takes twenty-nine runs. He switches to chords on his sixteenth and seems to be heading back to the vocals, but no! He bursts into single notes at the end of the twentieth run and keeps on going.

The following They Love Each Other slows the pace considerably, Garcia's solo as languid as the Mississippi River; it sounds like a Garcia Band treatment. Great.

Set three: during Scarlet Begonias, Garcia sounds a bit lost on the third run of his solo but pushes the envelope towards the end of the transition jam (7:55–9:05). At the end of the Terrapin Station outro, we get a new jam, mostly Brent and Drums.

Out of Space comes Truckin'. As one might expect, the "Busted! down on Bourbon Street" lyric gets a big cheer from the crowd. Wharf Rat has a beautiful middle section ("I'll get back, on my feet, someday"), Garcia and Brent summon gorgeous vocals.

Sugar Magnolia is given a crisp tempo, and Garcia's guitar tone has a chewy bite to it. On the main break, it seems his solo might run out of steam when the drummers kick it up ever so slightly; then Weir turns up the heat with his exciting, signature triplet-type chops (4:40–). It propels them into a big finish on a great inside break.

They forego the Sunshine Daydream half of the song in favor of Good Lovin'. It's a spirited version, Weir in his prime.

Encore: Brokedown Palace, a lovely stretch of strumming and singing. Sweet organ fills, earnest and melancholy vocals. Nearly just exactly perfect (alas, that half-second blip! and we could do with a quieter crowd as well).

Link to recordings

### 1981 BARCELONA, SPAIN
## SPORTS PALACE

Their third country in four days and the final gig of the European tour, with six weeks off ahead (though Garcia will start a Jerry Garcia Band tour within a week).

It sounds like they put everything they've got into this performance; Garcia plays all night with an endless supply of energy.

Jack Straw opens, Bill and Mickey kick it up on the tenth run in Garcia's solo. There is some great lead guitar work here, but none of the recordings capture it well. On Franklin's Tower, the fifth instrumental break is the best (10:21–). Just when you think the chording is simply ordinary, Garcia trills them hard and blasts off into more single note soloing (11:34–).

On Loser, he takes a truly original approach to the solo, throwing caution to the wind, playing notes that will land him god knows where. C.C. Rider has a fabulous organ solo by Brent, but, alas, there is Weir's slide.

During Let It Grow's main jam, Garcia begins to go supersonic (4:53–) then runs off on a wild romp (7:23–); you can hear Lesh going harder and lower beneath him. There's another, unexpected peak around the thirteen-minute mark, it's wonderful stuff.

Set two: on Scarlet Begonias, Garcia's sixth and last run is the best, all chords. The transition jam is fluid and driven, a great tempo and sustained invention here. Garcia surprisingly repeats the main Scarlet theme (11:00–), then it's back to jamming, including Brent's percussion-like tones.

They move on to Fire On The Mountain with some deliciously thick bass notes from Lesh. The first solo has curvy, winding bends and jet speed runs. On the second solo, Garcia plays with arpeggiated runs (5:58–), then breaks free and twitters atop a towering peak (6:22–6:30). Wow. The song finishes with the traditional descending theme, then more high-speed runs.

Saint Of Circumstance has a fantastic build to the climax (to quote Weir: "Ha!"). They end the song, but Garcia keeps on soloing, and it's not clear if anyone is going to join him. Mostly, it's just him running scales, toying with notes in the lowest register, switching on different tones. If you want to hear how fast Garcia's fingers once were, don't miss this. Some hand drumming begins around 2:45 and accompanies him the rest of the way.

After Garcia departs, Bill and Mickey have the stage to themselves for about five minutes. We get a bit of Space, then Spanish Jam and The Other One, both bright and shining, with additional maniacal soloing from Garcia. Brent creates great fills during the lily fields verse. They quiet down and manage to slow the pace, while Garcia begins to pick out lullaby-like notes (7:20–) and tiptoes into Stella Blue.

Sugar Magnolia closes, it's a powerful version. Garcia goes to chords during the inside break, never lets up, and then doubles down, even exploding into single-note soloing during Sunshine Daydream. Certainly, it's one of the best renditions ever.

Encore: Don't Ease Me In gets a similar treatment, raging.

1997 Deadbase respondents ranked this seventh best on the year (Headyversion ranks Sugar Magnolia eighteenth best all-time).

Link to recordings

## 1989 PHILADELPHIA, PA
## THE SPECTRUM

The second of three here, a rare Death Don't Have No Mercy appears at the end of set two, just their third version since the 9/29/89 revival (there would be only one more).

Help On The Way → Slipknot! opens set two, also recently resuscitated (10/8/89). Slipknot! gets the MIDI treatment. Franklin's Tower is solid, finishing a good starting sequence.

Estimated Prophet is up next. Brent plays lively through the verses, and Weir is quite animated. During the inside jam, after Garcia goes to chords and suggests we're nearing the end, he breaks out into a few more lines of single notes, a good thrill before returning to the vocals.

Some spacey-echoey MIDI effects start the Estimated Prophet outro jam. Brent takes off around 9:40, then it kind of comes to a halt a minute later and becomes more like Space, with Garcia going to his MIDI trumpet. They make a relatively smooth transition into Eyes Of The World, with more trumpet from Garcia in the final two minutes of the jam.

Death Don't Have No Mercy is a refreshing change of pace from the usual set enders, but this version does not have the power of the prior two examples, as we get just one run from Garcia on the solo break. Turn On Your Lovelight closes, their fourth cover tune in a row.

Encore: Baby Blue.

Deadbase respondents have this tied for tenth best of the year with 8/19/89 (the latter sounds more compelling).

Link to recordings

## 1990 BERLIN, GERMANY
## ICC BERLIN

This is the band's first and only visit to Berlin, they spend two nights here.

They open with Let The Good Times Roll, it's the first performance with the new crew (Vince, Bruce) (see 7/12/90). Hornsby takes the first verse, he's got an authentic late '50s/early '60s voice, a near dead ringer for Sam Cooke. Weir takes the next one, then Garcia.

They follow with Shakedown Street. A big blast from Lesh introduces it, it's always a treat to have extended improvisation early in the set. The jam starts with some call and response between Garcia, Hornsby, and Vince. Bill and Mickey kick it into higher gear and it starts to come together.

Set two has a good Fire On The Mountain; Garcia is solid on the vocals and guitar. At the end of the first break, we get some interesting piano (on the audience recording, you can hear Garcia trill chords underneath it, around 5:20).

Towards the end of Looks Like Rain, they quiet to just Weir and Drums, then they disappear, leaving only the crowd clapping. On Terrapin Station, Garcia misses the "which of you to gain me tell" verse. They go around twice led by the piano before tackling the next verse.

Wharf Rat is Hornsby's first ever with the band (guest or employee), and it's a tune that fits his piano playing like a glove. But he doesn't get much space to himself here and the drumming sounds a bit rushed on the back side.

Link to recordings


1994 NEW YORK CITY, NY

## MADISON SQUARE GARDEN

Their 52nd performance at this fabled venue (it would turn out to be their last). Long versions of Bird Song and Terrapin Station.

They open with Feel Like A Stranger. The jam is lengthy and well sustained, a big version befitting The Big Apple. Bertha is next, there is lots of rollicking energy here. If The Shoe Fits has a good groove but no home runs.

Bird Song closes the set. The jam starts to turn strange by the seven-minute mark, with Vince and Garcia both wandering into the weird. They get back onto the rails briefly until Vince goes chromatic again. It quiets around 11:30 and they won't be coalescing and building to the traditional major key peak, instead returning to the vocals. Garcia sings a "snow and rain" refrain with a "be with you" flavor. Fifteen minutes in all.

Set two features a twenty-three-minute Terrapin Station. There's a long inside jam after the "not to master" verse, wandering and dreamy, could it go somewhere else? (4:16–7:28). Garcia continues to shift his vocal accents ("counting *stars* by candlelight").

The "whistle is screaming" exit jam leaves the song behind in the final four or five minutes, ending with what is mostly Garcia and Drums. He sticks around for much of the Drums section.

Out of Space, it's Way To Go Home, one of the better new songs, a decent version, but then there's an odd transition to Stella Blue, not sewn together with jamming. It's still a beautiful ballad; the solo on the exit summons forever youthful notes.

Sugar Magnolia has the energy they started with tonight; Weir is supercharged.

Encore: Brokedown Palace, an apt end to what became their final concert in New York City (the 155th, starting with 6/1/67). Garcia uses his Corrina-like drone for the solo.

Link to recordings

# OCTOBER 20

1967 Studio
  (RCA in Los Angeles, or American in Hollywood)

1968 Berkeley, CA, University of California, Greek Theatre

1974 San Francisco, CA, Winterland Ballroom

1978 San Francisco, CA, Winterland Ballroom

1983 Worcester, MA, The Centrum

1984 Syracuse, NY, Syracuse University, Carrier Dome

1988 Houston, TX, The Summit

1989 Philadelphia, PA, The Spectrum

1990 Berlin, Germany, ICC Berlin

1967 STUDIO

A rehearsal with a handful of tunes (Lovelight, Alligator, Caution, Cryptical Envelopment, Viola Lee Blues). Pigpen sounds like a youngster on Lovelight, his voice in a slight echo chamber.

Link to recordings

 1968 BERKELEY, CA

## GREEK THEATER

This is their second performance at this venue; they won't be back until 9/11/81 (they will perform at the Berkeley Community Theatre in '71 and '72).

We have six songs including a ten-minute Dark Star. This one really captures Garcia's gorgeous tone in the lowest register of his guitar, as well as the classic motifs.

St. Stephen is completed in less than four minutes. Not much of an inside or outside jam, they go straight into the "high green chilly" lyrics.

The Eleven is as crisp and tight as you will ever hear it. Listen to Lesh start Caution while they are still inside the song. Pigpen stretches out with lively organ licks at the start before he goes down to see the gypsy woman. A great version, like a runaway locomotive, it's clear this is no ordinary band. "Feedback" begins around 9:45, the great grandpa of Space.

This should be considered among the best performances of 1968 (that we currently have). Headyversion voters rank Caution as tied for eighth best all-time.

Link to recordings

1974 SAN FRANCISCO, CA

## WINTERLAND BALLROOM

Their final concert (not!).

"As it should be on a Sunday night *in* San Francisco, The Grateful Dead." –BG

Three sets. Three encores. Their first Good Lovin' since 5/25/72. And Mickey Hart rejoins the band (see 1/25/71) for set two, most of set three, and the encores.

The first set is the strongest, before the toll of five straight performances (and perhaps other variables) takes effect.

Set two is a Playing In The Band sandwich filled with Drums, Not Fade Away, The Other One and Wharf Rat. We hear some fine jazz-flavored runs from Keith during the front end of the Playin' jam.

On Not Fade Away, there's a bit of a misstep as they start singing the "cadillac" verse then back off. They come around and take it from the top. After finishing the song, they begin The Other One, but a few measures in they yield to Drums.

The Other One goes quiet and spacey three minutes in. Coming out of the spacey part, around the six-minute mark, Garcia latches on to a motif and drives them back towards the main theme. The Spanish lady comes to Weir (8:24), but they skip the lily fields verse.

Wharf Rat is next. It's pretty, always poignant. There's no inside break, and the exit quickly morphs into a Playin'-style jam to finish the set.

Set three opens with Good Lovin'. The harmony vocals are a bit rough, understandably, and it's hard to tell if what follows is supposed to be an extended jam or just a solo break over the verses. It turns out to be the latter, for the most part. Lesh sounds like he wants to break into a "Feelin' Groovy" jam. They are making it up as they go.

Five minutes into it, the jam is led by Keith and Lesh. Around 6:30, Garcia plays slide. They return to the theme and vocals at the ten-minute mark.

Eyes Of The World gets its third reading on this stand. It starts with a bit of a Lesh solo. On the first break, it sounds like Garcia is running out of gas, though he's stronger on the second. The third break is the Lesh solo. Around the fourteen-minute mark, you can hear Garcia begin to pencil out Slipknot!

There's a classic Stella Blue, pin-drop quiet, sparse instrumentation, Garcia's clean, youthful voice. They close with Sugar Magnolia, played for the second straight night. On the exit jam, Garcia seems quite low in the mix; it's hard to detect much of a solo.

Triple encore: Lesh reintroduces Mickey Hart to the crowd, and Weir explains: "Fresh out of the mental institution in a brand-new band. He still has uncontrollable urges to throw things."

Johnny B. Goode, Mississippi Half Step, and We Bid You Goodnight follow.

That's all folks (until 3/23/75).

Link to recordings

## 1978 SAN FRANCISCO, CA

# WINTERLAND BALLROOM

Their third of five on this stand. The double encore features Shakedown Street, just their third performance of the song. Dancin' In The Streets is positioned right before Drums, a twenty-minute version.

They open with Minglewood Blues, it's not a high-powered rendition. Keith's solo is two runs, then Weir's slide which is mainly a curiosity at this point with just one run. The highlight of set one may be Tennessee Jed, Garcia generates real excitement in his solo.

There are some fireworks in set two on Franklin's Tower. On the "listen to the music play" break, Garcia drills his chords and Weir joins him with his own. Later, more triplets from Weir (9:45) and rolling thunder from Garcia finish it off.

The rest is uneventful. There's not much of note in the Dancin' In The Streets jam. They pick up the pace a bit after eight minutes, but the stars don't seem to be aligned; there's no magic here. By eleven minutes, it's nap time. Really.

At the fourteen-minute mark it sounds like they are still fidgeting, devolving into Space after seventeen minutes, Weir's slide a main contributor. They suddenly snap out of it (18:25) with some wobbling from Garcia and a straight-ahead beat from the drummers. But there will be no return to the theme or the vocals, just Drums.

Near the end of Not Fade Away, Garcia begins to play the Black Peter lick, but it takes a while before Bill and Mickey give way, it's not a slick transition. On the outro jam, Weir's slide is nearly as high in the mix as Garcia's guitar for most of it. Around And Around is another one where the instrumental break kind of falls flat; Garcia is not quite firing on all cylinders.

Deadbase respondents in '97 had this tied for eleventh best on the year (that seems generous; several April performances they ranked lower deserve promotion, such as 4/11/78 and 4/12/78). If you are looking for brilliant renditions of some of these songs (Half Step, Franklin's, Dancin', Shakedown) in the vicinity of this time frame, see 11/23/78.

Link to recordings

## 1983 WORCESTER, MA
# THE CENTRUM

This is the first night of two at a venue new to the band. There is energy in abundance, along with several mishaps.

In set two, Help On The Way has a fast tempo that's a bit much for the vocals. But what a fit for Slipknot!, a high-powered version; Garcia hits the heights. Franklin's Tower is also frenzied, they're still in high gear on the final break, with Weir furiously ringing his chords.

There's no ballad next. Bill and Mickey launch Samson & Delilah before Garcia has put the finishing touches on his Franklin's coda. But then…where's Weir?

They literally bring the Samson intro to a halt after a minute, then start the song up again. Later, Garcia delivers a truly funky lick that goes sideways (6:18–6:22), either a slip or sleight of hand.

After an interesting rendering of The Other One, Garcia muffs the first verse of Stella Blue, going silent after two lines. They come around several times, but Garcia is still not ready, the broken angel wandering until he's able to recall that "all the years combine." (2:46)

There's a nice recovery during his spotlight moment, Bill and Mickey rolling out the red carpet for the "blue light, cheap hotel" refrain. Garcia gives new accents to several words here, and follows one of them— "tryin'"—with a nifty fill (see also Eyes Of The World for more of this treatment). The outro solo is filled with tender notes; it's achingly beautiful.

The transition between Around And Around and Good Lovin' is a mess, and they have trouble getting the rhythm started right, but the closer ends well. There's a particularly passionate Good Lovin' rap from Weir, with the audience pitching in.

Encore: Day Job, a decent version, bright and bouncy, with the kind of chord changes and soloing (one run) that should endear themselves. But many can't stomach the lyrics.

Worth a full listen, Deadbase respondents much prefer the next night, 10/21/83.

Link to recordings

## 1984 SYRACUSE, NY
# SYRACUSE UNIVERSITY, CARRIER DOME

"These kids up here are lookin' plenty bug-eyed." –BW

Amidst the first set, that's Weir's second warning about the crush up front, the fire marshal apparently considering a shutdown. You can hear that Weir is upset and losing patience. Despite the melee, or perhaps because of it, there are some charged performances here.

Jack Straw is one of those, it closes the first set. You can hear the ire in Weir's vocals in the first verses: "…cut down a man in *cold* blood…might as well be…*me!*" Garcia follows with a rare trilling of chords in his very first fill. The outro features a potential record-setting thirty-three runs, with several highlights: Garcia going to chords (13th); Lesh's first bomb (20th); and Garcia's final fill after the "morning light" line.

"We're gonna take a short break, we'll be right back, everybody move back." –BW

Set two starts with a more official announcement threatening to halt the concert unless people on the floor retreat. Fortunately, the crowd is able to comply, and the band opens with Shakedown Street.

The "just gotta poke around" refrain has more of those surprisingly energetic Garcia fills, and a propulsive jam ensues. An echo device is added to the final vocals, and before you can blink, they begin Samson & Delilah.

He's Gone has a divine inside solo, uniquely inspired, fearless, two runs. Even the blind and dirty vocals occasionally shine. They seamlessly shift from the "nothing's gonna bring him back" vocals into their second Smokestack Lightning since the revival (10/9/84). Brent plays some jazzy descending chords (3:30) that seem to fit, but Weir has something else going on.

Suddenly, they drop all that and run off to gosh knows where. Bill and Mickey put out a beat that could work for Goin' Down The Road, but their creation keeps shedding its skin, becoming a special, surprising Jam (4:00–7:55).

The Other One is tight and crisp, Garcia soars. The inside jam is one you think may end, but they keep pushing. Then they go from the lily fields to Black Peter in less than thirty seconds. They're in the pocket here, Garcia's ragged vocals a perfect fit, Brent's organ underneath, lucid soloing.

They end the concert with Turn On Your Lovelight, still a rarity at this time (the last time they closed with it was 8/6/71). This one is not just nostalgic, though, they turn up the intensity on the jam (3:30–) and find their fifth gear.

Encore: Revolution (#6).

This concert did not make the respondents' top twenty for the year (Deadbase X). It would likely rank higher if surveyed today (Heady-version voters rank Jack Straw fifth best all-time).

Link to recordings

## 1988 HOUSTON, TX

# THE SUMMIT

After a day off, they pull in from New Orleans for one here. Tonight is their first performance of Built To Last.

China Cat Sunflower opens set two, and there is decent jamming in I Know You Rider. On the following Playing In The Band, Weir sings strongly, but the jam kind of fizzles out after six minutes.

The new song, Built To Last, begins quickly on its heels; it features a three-chord, punchy motif strikingly similar to Rubin & Cherise, and a cadence that resembles the two-year-old Black Muddy River. The final minute starts out like a unique Jam. Weir puts on a special effect, but it ends too soon as they hang it up for Drums.

Before Space is done, Garcia starts up I Need A Miracle, Weir eventually joins. The crowd is in full voice, finishing Weir's chorus (3:00–). The outro jam lasts just a handful of bars before a pivot into Dear Mr. Fantasy. It's passionately sung by Brent, with several high-flying runs from Garcia on his solos, but it's hard to fully appreciate on the available recordings.

Link to recordings

## 1989 PHILADELPHIA, PA
## THE SPECTRUM

The play-all-night set two stretches nearly two hours, including a long Other One Jam (see 8/13/75) and a full, ten-minute The Other One.

They close set one with California Earthquake, a Rodney Crowell ballad sung a bit like Standing On The Moon, in recognition of the October 17 Loma Prieta, California, quake.

Hey Pocky Way opens set two, and as always it is one of the best showcases for Brent's soloing.

On Truckin', the exit jam is brief as Garcia begins to play with the Other One theme. Around the three-minute mark he switches to MIDI flute. After five minutes, there's a rogue musical streak across the sky. The jam swallows the red pill and the sound effects kick in. Garcia reaches out to grab the main Other One theme (10:35) and continues to fiddle with it, but they disappear into Drums without a word from the Spanish lady.

Post-Space, after Brent's I Will Take You Home, they begin to jam in Other One territory. After the Spanish lady verse, Garcia's MIDI becomes a bassoon.

Wharf Rat has a two-minute meandering intro, with a less-than-great inside jam that feels disjointed. On the closing Sugar Magnolia, Garcia doesn't do much on the inside jam. Brent is the bright spot here; it's interesting to hear him team up with Weir at the start of the Sunshine Daydream vocals.

Encore: Brokedown Palace.

Link to recordings

## 1990 BERLIN, GERMANY
# ICC BERLIN

The band cooks up a unique Jam after Let It Grow and performs their fourth Dark Star of the year.

At the end of Let It Grow, the song dissolves into sparse notes and a spacey chorale led by Hornsby. After some pretty single note runs (1:30–), he has it all to himself a minute later. It's the kind of thing that could easily have shifted into his song The Way It Is, but he invents a different melody, then flies off. After a brief pause, we get Box Of Rain, a lovely way to end the set.

Set two features an interesting transition from Eyes Of The World into Samson & Delilah. Bill and Mickey set the Samson beat late in Eyes, but the rest of the crew briefly holsters their instruments before making the transition.

Ship Of Fools has major vocal flubs in the second verse ("I won't leave you—"), and the tempo sounds jacked up. The song is played as a shuffle, with skating rink keyboard sounds instead of, say, low-key nightclub piano.

It's a great surprise to hear Dark Star next. After eight minutes, it begins a long slide into free jamming. Drums and Space follow, then we get a bit more of Dark Star, including verse two.

Link to recordings

# OCTOBER 21

1966 San Francisco, CA, Fillmore Auditorium
(no setlist, no recording)

1968 San Francisco, CA, Jefferson Airplane House
(setlist, no recording)

1971 Chicago, IL, Auditorium Theater

1972 Nashville, TN, Vanderbilt University, Alumni Lawn

1973 Omaha, NE, Civic Auditorium

1978 San Francisco, CA, Winterland Ballroom

1983 Worcester, MA, The Centrum

1988 Dallas, TX, Reunion Arena

## 1971 CHICAGO, IL
# AUDITORIUM THEATER

"Thank you, sports fans." –PL

It's Keith's second outing and he's everywhere, a veritable Godchaux highlight reel. You can hear him upfront on the very first number, Truckin', pouncing and percussive. He's all over the next one, Loser, and on so many others, from pounding out late '50s rock 'n' roll chords on Beat It On Down The Line and Big Railroad Blues, to avant-garde lines in his first Dark Star.

Dark Star bats fourth in set two, and it's Keith who steers it into an atonal lane with his rising series of chromatic notes (3:00–). They wander far and wide, a caravan through the cosmos, until Garcia picks up the main theme again (5:25–). After verse one, it's starry skies of slow, twinkling notes until they catch a comet (11:33–).

Garcia bursts into "Feelin' Groovy"-like licks (13:00–),then it's back down the rabbit hole when suddenly they step through the doors of an Appalachian barn and start a rollicking version of Sitting On Top Of The World (the only example of this segue). Just as quickly, they move on and summon the Dark Star theme, and we get the "mirror shatters" verse before an exit into Me & Bobby McGee.

Double encore: a rare standalone St. Stephen (there are vocal flubs, and massive bass blasts to start the jam), and an equally rare answer to The Answer Man: Johnny B. Goode.

This show was not among the Deadbase respondents' top twenty in 1997 but is perhaps a must-listen for Keith's contributions; probably one of his best outings. Great.

Link to recordings

1972 NASHVILLE, TN

## VANDERBILT UNIVERSITY, ALUMNI LAWN

We have six songs from this concert starting mid-set two with He's Gone through Morning Dew.

Lesh is up in the mix, a fine chance to hear his creative choice of notes and innovative slides in He's Gone. Garcia quotes from First There Is A Mountain during the exit jam (11:45–). Weir ends with a descending pattern vaguely recalling Tennessee Jed.

Truckin' features a particularly fiery solo from Garcia, a hallmark of his work during this year. After six minutes, they take it down to a lower boil, then ratchet it back up a few minutes later, another marvelous opportunity to hear Lesh upfront. This jam carries an Other One flavor, and that's where it goes.

Four minutes in, Weir sounds absent. Further along, there's a short descending passage that might remind you of Slipknot! (8:18–); at this point, it's still waiting to be born. Garcia and Lesh rediscover the main Other One theme simultaneously around 10:35, then the Spanish lady verse comes at 11:42. They descend into the underworld, Garcia twirling backwards, Lesh blasting atonal aspersions.

They seem to skip the lily fields verse and then transition into Morning Dew. Here you can finally hear Weir's guitar and just a bit of Keith's piano on the "guess it doesn't matter" refrain, but it's Lesh's axe that takes the cake. Garcia brings his stampeding chords, once through (11:25).

Your ears will anticipate the comforting strains of Sugar Magnolia, the perfect antidote to the apocalypse, but alas the tape runs dry.

Link to recordings

1973 OMAHA, NE

## CIVIC AUDITORIUM

"Wait a minute. We gotta teach our drummer to count to twenty." –BW

Weir himself has trouble counting while trying to announce the correct score of the deciding game of the World Series (Oakland 5, New York 2), perhaps a harbinger of missteps to come ("we gotta fix the piano again").

Tonight's highlight is the Playing In The Band sandwich in set two, thirty-two minutes' worth, featuring the detour into Mississippi Half Step and then Big River.

The lowlights include the blown start to Beat It On Down The Line, and a rare bungled bridge in Loser (1:40) (Garcia starts the "last fair deal" verse, but the rest of the band is asleep at the switch.) His singing also sounds shaky here.

There's a good Playing In The Band jam, with no hint that Mississippi Half Step is ahead. The exit from there into Big River is largely triggered by Lesh. You'll hear an amazing ending to that song, a magic moment that transports them back into Playing In The Band. Amidst the revived Playin' jam, Lesh suddenly announces his authority (4:45–) and from there it quiets in both tempo and tone.

During the Truckin' jam, Keith digs in and forces a change in direction (8:50–). Garcia closes the door on it and walks his way into Wharf Rat. He sings the middle part of the song—"But I'll get back…"—nearly acapella. After nine minutes, he starts some supreme noodling.

Set one ends with Weather Report Suite, parts one and two are picture perfect. Let It Grow is crisp, all parts in sync, quite good. Keith lends it a jazz flavor after 7:30, Garcia lets fly a small warble without breaking stride (8:00–8:02).

Link to recordings

## 1978 SAN FRANCISCO, CA
# WINTERLAND BALLROOM

This is their fourth outing on this five-night stand.

Hamza El Din is the opening act, singing on two shorter pieces and then delivering an eighteen-minute Ollin Arageed (#4) that is mostly an instrumental. When he sings the melody, Garcia accompanies him on guitar. The rest of the band joins for the final minute or two and it morphs into a bit of a jam, with a nifty segue into Promised Land. Yes, Nubian folk jammed into Chuck Berry.

Garcia seems on his game from the start, taking flight with a high-pitched fill while Weir is still singing about "the terminal gate," then exploding on his final three runs with trilled chords.

During the set two Got My Mojo Working, Weir cooks up a Dancin' In The Streets-like chord pattern that sounds similar to the Bee Gees' Stayin' Alive (2:25–). When Lee Oskar's harmonica kicks in, you can imagine Pigpen stepping up to the microphone and telling you about a gypsy woman. But instead, we get Weir singing the song, followed by Garcia's brief Minglewood-style soloing. On his next run, he pulls out his slide. Later, Weir does the same.

From there, they coordinate a slick transition into The Other One. A short version, it seems to be nothing special until we get to the lily fields. Before that verse there are sky-high bends from Garcia, then an ear-splitting rise (6:10–) and thundering power chords.

The Stella Blue exit jam has more fireworks, the nearly great solo finishes with Morning Dew-like flourishes, surprisingly massive.

There are other treats, such as Garcia's stirring inside solo on Estimated Prophet.

(Headyversion voters rank this Stella Blue best all-time, by a wide margin).

Link to recordings

## 1983 WORCESTER, MA
## THE CENTRUM

A big set two on Brent's first birthday performance with the band. Four lengthy songs before Drums, plus a fifteen-minute Space featuring a Garcia-Weir duet of sorts.

Scarlet Begonias opens set two. Around the ten-minute mark, something lights a fire under Garcia and the jam heats up. It's worth the wait, several minutes of passionate seeking.

There's a long intro to Fire On The Mountain. We don't hear Garcia's double-noted theme until two minutes in; the first verse comes at 3:15. The initial instrumental break has Silly Putty guitar bends, then high-speed sprints.

Uncle John's Band follows, it's a solid version. The Playing In The Band jam starts in near silence, just Garcia and drumbeats. There's some interesting stuff from Weir around the eight-minute mark and more of the same later, a unique version that ends in a rainforest shower of cymbals.

Drums begins with synthesized shooting stars, then sticks. Halfway through, intense thwacking, like construction work on a big-city sidewalk.

Space starts with Garcia's low-toned Close Encounters sound, but it quickly morphs into something else. Weir joins; his whammy bar is prominent around the three-minute mark. Then we briefly hear some licks from him that recall Sage & Spirit (there are more of those near the five-minute mark).

After that, it's mostly Garcia on his own, throwing off some rising Slip-knot!-like licks, and later his own Sage & Spirit-type stuff (9:45ish). He's soon ready to move on into Truckin' or something else.

Link to recordings

## 1988 DALLAS, TX
# REUNION ARENA

This is the final gig on this mini-tour, and in hindsight their last show in the state of Texas. Brent gets a birthday greeting at the start of set two. Tonight's songs include a rarity, a revival, and many of the newer ones.

After a Let The Good Times Roll aperitif, they get into the first set with Feel Like A Stranger (their last visit to Dallas was ten years ago, 12/22/78).

Mid-set they play Believe It Or Not (#6 of seven); fans won't see it again until 3/22/90. A rare Dupree's Diamond Blues appears near the end of the set; it was performed just three times this year (then once in '89, '90, and '94). Garcia handles the vocal duties better here than on the Franklin's Tower earlier in the set.

Set two opens with Wang Dang Doodle, revived after two and a half years; it will become a regular through 1995.

Victim Or The Crime is next, there's an interesting jam that shows potential before they move quickly into Foolish Heart. There are some vocal struggles on the latter, but Garcia strengthens on the next-to-final refrain, then Brent joins and injects some wonderful keyboard energy. The jam sounds like it will fade out (9:15–), but they persist and rebuild for one more vocal chorus and a celebratory finish. A decent, lengthy version (over eleven minutes).

There are five songs post-Drums. On Stella Blue, Garcia finds a pretty phrase and elevates the exit jam. Then we get a mess in Sugar Magnolia: after the "Cajun rhythm" verse, Weir skips ahead past "ringin' that bluebell," so he's singing one thing and Garcia is playing another. Ouch.

Encore: Brokedown Palace.

Link to recordings

# OCTOBER 22

1966 San Francisco, CA, Fillmore Auditorium
(no setlist, no recording)

1967 San Francisco, CA, Winterland Ballroom

1971 Chicago, IL, Auditorium Theater

1978 San Francisco, CA, Winterland Ballroom

1980 New York City, NY, Radio City Music Hall

1983 Syracuse, NY, Syracuse University, Carrier Dome

1989 Charlotte, NC, Charlotte Coliseum

1990 Frankfurt, Germany, Festhalle

1967 SAN FRANCISCO, CA

## WINTERLAND BALLROOM

We have seven songs, including what appears to be the earliest live recording of That's It For The Other One.

New Potato Caboose is perhaps the fourth rendition we know of. Garcia's blues-rock licks here sound a lot like the Allman Brothers will in a couple of years (4:30–). Lesh's bass and Pigpen's organ are powerful stuff. They build to another stomping peak around the nine-minute mark.

Cryptical Envelopment, the dreamy, carnival organ sounds (The Doors? Procol Harum?) soon yield to the central lick in The Other One. Pile-driven by Lesh in subsequent versions, this one is introduced by Garcia's raunchy guitar and Pigpen's organ.

Amidst the jam, we hear what might be one of Garcia's earliest stuttering warbles (2:41–2:58), then the initial verse, sung by Weir: "When I woke up this morning, my head was not attached…" No Spanish lady, no lily fields, but the heat does come 'round, the only lyric in this rendition that survives.

The back end of Cryptical goes nearly nine minutes, starting with Lesh's fountaining, descending bass licks underneath. Garcia takes off on his flying Irish jig (6:02–), the jam a swirling psychedelic stew that builds to a shattering climax.

Turn On Your Lovelight is also compelling, the second earliest recording of this tune available. Garcia's E-major licks could be right at home in the Allman's Blue Sky four years hence. Snappy drums, and some rapping from Pigpen. After twelve minutes, Lesh steps into the fray.

Link to recordings

1971 CHICAGO, IL

## AUDITORIUM THEATER

Their second night here features a near thirty-minute That's It For The Other One.

Another fine night for Keith, e.g., great western saloon-style piano on Me & My Uncle.

Cryptical Envelopment begins plaintively, with that folksy *Aoxomoxoa* feeling, before five minutes of drumming. Lesh begins The Other One with his rocketing bass propellant (7:33–). After eleven minutes, the jam begins to coalesce, all their lines coming together, gathering strength and then exploding. There is a stunning entrance to the first verse.

They keep it on full boil until minute fourteen when it begins to calm, and suddenly we're not in Illinois anymore. Mysteries dark and vast surface but without heavy dissonance. Garcia begins to play with the theme again around the twenty-minute mark. Keith finds an interesting figure (21:30–) and that mini-jam fades, too. Lesh decides it's time to head home; several blasts of his bass and they are rambling down the road again.

After the lily fields, there's a short Cryptical jam to finish, low-key improv over the two chords (A-G), with a seamless, natural segue into Deal (key of A).

Link to recordings

1978 SAN FRANCISCO, CA

# WINTERLAND BALLROOM

"They're not the best at what they do, they're the only ones that do what they do, The Grateful Dead." –BG

Their fifth concert here in six nights and the wear is starting to show. The performance sounds a bit loose in places and is somewhat lagging.

After Ollin Arageed, they need extra effort to transition into Deal. Later, Garcia seems to lose his vocal place, he's very late on the final verse (4:15–4:30).

Jack Straw closes set one, there is some strong singing from Weir here. After the first jam and the "he don't go home with all" lyric, he holds the final word aloft for an eternity (4:55–5:01).

Scarlet Begonias opens set two, it has a typical inside jam of three runs, the following transition jam is subdued. Fire On The Mountain has a shy, tentative start, Weir's slide is on the last two breaks; Garcia has some fine flourishes during the final minute.

Not Fade Away is mostly forgettable. After seventeen minutes, Weir leads them into a Mojo Workin' Jam, Garcia playing single notes over some Mind Left Body descending chords. During Goin' Down The Road, only Garcia's final solo run is a rouser, but they finish strong.

Deadbase respondents in '97 had this fifth best of the year and tied with the prior night, a miss on both counts (hard to fathom this one getting five times the votes of 2/5/78 and 11/20/78, and 2/3/78 receiving none).

Link to recordings

1980 NEW YORK CITY, NY

## RADIO CITY MUSIC HALL

This is the band's debut at this fabled venue, the first of eight performances here over the next thirteen nights. They will perform one acoustic set and two electric sets as at the Warfield and Saenger.

The first electric set gets off to a blistering start. Alabama Getaway has a shot of New York energy. The set ends with a good China Cat → Rider, Garcia on his game; there's great soloing in the final minute of the jam before they enter I Know You Rider. After Weir's "march winds" verse, they take an instrumental break, with two runs for Garcia (this arrangement later disappeared, as they would do Weir's verse and Garcia's "headlight" verse back-to-back). Great final break.

The final set of the night opens with Scarlet Begonias. There's a fine finish to Garcia's third inside solo run: chords, a run up the hill, then a hockey stop on musical skates. He's having some fun with the vocals, too ("everybody's *play*-ay-a-ying…"). The following jam is just a few minutes old before they segue into Fire On The Mountain, a relatively short version.

The real fireworks are in the Saint Of Circumstance inside break; listen for the hair-raising crescendo (you will need to add quite a bit of volume to the recording(s) to get a sense of it).

Post-Drums they end Not Fade Away in a dead stop, then start up Goin' Down The Road. Well played, Garcia still firing on all cylinders, they work it into a lively Good Lovin' for the finish.

Link to recordings

1983 SYRACUSE, NY

# SYRACUSE UNIVERSITY, CARRIER DOME

The band travels 273 miles west for their Saturday night performance here. They experience none of the crowd control issues they'll have when they come back next year (10/20/84).

Shakedown Street starts set one. The band sounds tight, the jam is pretty good. They follow with an early Wang Dang Doodle (#6). It sounds like a youngster; Weir bites off the lyrics and Garcia gets two solos. It fell out of the repertoire in 1985, and again in 1987, but became a regular in 1989.

On Bird Song, Lesh is up in the mix, spinning his own lengthy lines alongside Garcia's. After six minutes, Garcia engages his extra gear, unleashing a series of fast dashes. Weir steps up before we hear the theme and they return to the vocals.

In set two, after Terrapin Station, Weir and the drummers begin a new Jam (13:25–). Call it Weir & Drums, a good one, with compelling chording.

Drums → Space runs about twenty-five minutes, unusually long for this time frame. The final five minutes contains a compelling Garcia-Weir duet, with hints of If I Had The World To Give from the lead guitar, and Spanish Jam-like sounds out of the rhythm guitar.

A long intro to The Wheel follows, Garcia works up a new motif before breaking into song. Throwing Stones has fancy, sliding licks from Garcia at the start of the jam, with Weir slashing like a samurai, then wielding his triplet chords.

On Not Fade Away, Garcia is still on the mark. Amidst the crowd's song-ending chant, Weir starts up a too-fast version of One More Saturday Night.

Encore: Revolution (#3).

Link to recordings

## 1989 CHARLOTTE, NC
# CHARLOTTE COLISEUM

Their first visit to this city in five years, they deliver Help On The Way → Slipknot! → Franklin's Tower after two songs in set two, featuring a unique post-Franklin's session of sound effects.

The fourth of five renditions of Help On The Way → Slipknot! this year after a four-year layoff, this one hits the mark, revealing it to be well suited to Garcia's Wolf-MIDI setup. The last three minutes of Slipknot! we get Garcia's oboe (it sounds richer/deeper on the audience recording, more bassoon-like).

Franklin's Tower seems like it will end after eight minutes, but Garcia keeps noodling on a figure, the crowd roars, and they don't leave the stage, eventually pasting together a collage of sounds, all Space with no Jam.

The first set has a few wrinkles as well, such as a Foolish Heart opener (they'd open with that just once more), and a Johnny B. Goode closer.

Deadbase respondents rate half a dozen other October performances higher.

Link to recordings

## FESTHALLE

A Bruce Hornsby song gets a prime spot: The Valley Road closes set one in its debut. Well placed, it has an upbeat bounce like the Beatles' Revolution (that one was last covered by the band on 3/28/90).

Set two has an interesting percussion intro to Victim Or The Crime (0:30–1:04). The end of the jam has carpeted hall motorcycle, a swirl of Mr. Kite's keyboards, and swishing cymbals.

Before Drums, we get Uncle John's Band. In the second D minor jam, Garcia briefly re-touches the Playing In The Band theme, but they quickly move on to uncharted areas. Later, there are some pretty, descending lines from Lesh (10:00–).

Encore: The Weight (#9). The vocals are taken in this order: Garcia, Hornsby, Lesh, Weir then the last one is shared. Some nice piano licks are sprinkled throughout.

Link to recordings

# OCTOBER 23

1966 Walnut Creek, CA, Las Lomas High School
(no setlist, no recording)

1970 Washington, DC, Georgetown University,
McDonough Arena

1971 Detroit, MI, Eastown Theatre

1972 Milwaukee, WI, Performing Arts Center

1973 Bloomington, MN, Metropolitan Sports Center

1980 New York City, NY, Radio City Music Hall

1989 Charlotte, NC, Charlotte Coliseum

1970 WASHINGTON, DC

# GEORGETOWN UNIVERSITY, MCDONOUGH ARENA

The band's first visit to the nation's capital.

An early Truckin' (#8?), Weir sings one "get back, Truckin' on" before Garcia takes the baton and leads an exit jam that is pleasant but a long way from the furious rager it would become in the next year. They shift seamlessly into The Other One (no Cryptical Envelopment here), and the Spanish lady verse comes quickly.

They stir an equally smooth segue from the Other One jam into Not Fade Away. A very early Goin' Down The Road follows (#4?) with Garcia's Bid You Goodnight coda. He takes two runs and each one chases its own tail for a while. They feel their way back into Not Fade.

There are some good Weir guitar moments, such as his extended solo in Hard To Handle (2:34–4:11) (stick around for the ensuing weave highlighting Garcia and Lesh), and his lead on the China Cat jam.

Link to recordings

1971 DETROIT, MI

# EASTOWN THEATRE

Not Fade Away contains a thrilling jam (2:30–). Lesh is up in the mix and matching Garcia stride for stride. It quiets after a couple of minutes, then Lesh turns up the heat and throws in St. Stephen chords (D-A) for a couple of measures. Garcia starts feeling it, too, and breaks into flight, a series of cascading pull-offs (6:05–).

Similar flights of fancy abound on Goin' Down The Road. On the ending coda, they stretch it out, Lesh playing Cold Rain & Snow lines and Garcia hunkering down on a repeating pattern, before going back into Not Fade Away.

There is plenty of good playing elsewhere. Cumberland Blues is bright and bouncy, one of a run of fourteen straight they did (8/6/71 through 10/27/71). Truckin' is a standalone version. They return to the vocals after a long jam (they have yet to create the rising crescendo that will be the centerpiece of later versions).

No encore.

"OK, The Grateful Dead'll be back in tomorrow night, don't miss 'em."

Link to recordings

## 1972 MILWAUKEE, WI
## PERFORMING ARTS CENTER

Tonight's main course is a twenty-eight-minute Dark Star. A grand gallivant, the first verse is still off in the distance ten minutes in. Garcia revisits and plays with the descending theme (11:47 –), and a minute later Dark Star crashes.

There's no letdown from there. Bill keeps the pace, though the notes turn a bit darker and atonal by sixteen minutes and quite dissonant several minutes later, Garcia spinning and sputtering out of control. It becomes a dark and haunted house of disharmony, finally calming around the twenty-five minute mark.

It finishes with beautiful, lonesome tones from an underworldly fiddler, quieting to nothingness. Out of that void, a surprising, happy segue into Mississippi Half Step (#19). You can hear Donna on the "Rio Grandio" chorus, then some soloing before they return to sing the chorus again. Barely taking a breath, they begin Me & Bobby McGee.

Set one has a rare Rockin' Pneumonia, their fifth and final version (see 5/23/72), Keith gets a solo here. After some comments from Weir about "even numbers," they launch a lengthy Playing In The Band to close the set. An urgent, propulsive, cerebral exploration, they shift into a slightly lower gear after ten minutes. When they return to the theme and chorus, the band is joined by spirited clapping in time from the crowd. Fabulous.

Link to recordings

## 1973 BLOOMINGTON, MN
# METROPOLITAN SPORTS CENTER

All's well here except the end, an ugly incident between security and a fan amidst the first encore, a literal showstopper ("Everybody quit throwin' punches and we'll start playin' again." –BW).

There's a unique sound tonight coming from Keith's hands, starting on Black Throated Wind, an organ tone like a hockey rink's Wurlitzer. He's back on piano for the following Loose Lucy.

Truckin' opens set two, we get Keith's piano fills and then that Wurlitzer again (2:35–). Nobody's Fault But Mine noodlings begin in the final minute; they jam on that theme quietly for awhile then wander off. Garcia's playing is fluid, he spins serpentine lines and then finds a couple of new motifs along the way towards The Other One. The Spanish lady verse comes after six minutes. They slow the bus, pull over, and drift with the musical current until Bill begins a short drum solo.

What's next is what should be called Space. Lesh rumbles, Garcia pulls out his slide for some mournful, lonesome licks, and Weir later pings harmonics. It's a Zen garden of sounds, giving rise to Weir's beautiful classical chords that begin Weather Report Suite. Keith takes a sparkling piano solo in the WRS jam (12:24–).

The encore becomes an enfant terrible. Casey Jones starts off decently, then amidst the third chorus ("trouble behind"), the music halts and Lesh goes ballistic at the sight of the violence ("OK! OK! OK asshole! OK asshole! OK asshole! That's it for you!…).

It takes nearly three minutes to restore order, and the band decides to play on, delivering One More Saturday Night.

(The sound check has what sounds like an instrumental Wang Dang Doodle. You can hear it in the melody line on Garcia's guitar, 1:10–, and later; for their first official version visit 8/26/83).

Link to recordings

1980 NEW YORK CITY, NY

## RADIO CITY MUSIC HALL

The band's second night here. A fine, well-balanced acoustic set and two relatively mellow electric sets.

Set one has an upbeat start with On The Road Again, then the tried-and-true It Must Have Been The Roses. On Dark Hollow, Garcia gets two solo breaks, with two runs on the second. During Jack A Roe his soloing sounds focused and crisp. It's even better on Cassidy, stuttering, staccato lines during the jam, then the band makes a smooth return to the vocals. The first words in China Doll—"A pistol shot…"—send the crowd into a New York roar.

Electric set one: the opening Feel Like A Stranger is on low boil start to finish. They fill the setlist with mid-tempo numbers. Only the closing Music Never Stopped has the stuffing to raise the roof, but even that one is tame. On Big Railroad Blues, Garcia takes just two runs on his first solo, and three on the next, an AM radio version (3:27) (Cf. 9/2/83).

The final set is better. Some sparks fly on the inside jam of Estimated Prophet, though Garcia doesn't quite nail the landing. Terrapin Station has a boisterous but short exit jam. Truckin' and Sugar Magnolia are among the final songs, an *American Beauty* greatest hits parade.

Encore: Casey Jones.

Link to recordings

## 1989 CHARLOTTE, NC
# CHARLOTTE COLISEUM

The Golden State's troubles still on their mind, California Earthquake opens set one. The encore is Attics of My Life, their third rendition after seventeen years of hibernation.

After the quake song, we get Feel Like A Stranger, Brent's heavy synth is present on the chorus, a foreshadow of Vince's sound. Even stranger is Garcia's MIDI midway through the jam (5:03–). On Walking Blues, Brent scat sings briefly alongside the first run of his organ solo.

Bertha gets a rare mid-set position. Brent joins Garcia on the "jail-house" verse, then provides occasional violin fills on When I Paint My Masterpiece.

They close with Let It Grow. After a moment's hesitation in the first break, Garcia engages his trumpet sound (3:24).

Set two has a decidedly low-key pre-Drums section, from Looks Like Rain to We Can Run, Crazy Fingers to Terrapin Station.

They pause before launching We Can Run (#16 of twenty-two), Brent's piano voicings sounding a bit like Hornsby. Garcia's first guitar line recalls Black Muddy River. Brent pulls a major blank on the second verse, and they have to go around twice before he's ready to start the "dumpin' my trash" verse.

Terrapin delivers the most punch, it has an upbeat pace. It has a long exit jam (8:27–15:01) that's all Terrapin-themed but for the last twenty seconds.

Link to recordings

# OCTOBER 24

1969 San Francisco, CA, Winterland Ballroom

1970 St. Louis, MO, Kiel Opera House

1971 Detroit, MI, Eastown Theater

1972 Milwaukee, WI, Performing Arts Center

1979 Springfield, MA, Springfield Civic Center

1990 Hamburg, Germany, Sporthalle Hamburg

1969 SAN FRANCISCO, CA

## WINTERLAND BALLROOM

The first of three straight here, the recordings capture eight songs.

The currently less viewed recording has the lily fields verse from The Other One and the back end of Cryptical Envelopment (a total of less than four minutes from the full suite). At the end of Cryptical, there's an amazing, hair-raising, two-minute entrance into Cosmic Charlie.

China Cat Sunflower and I Know You Rider are coupled here, perhaps for the third time (see 7/5/69 and 9/30/69). The transition jam runs a bit over a minute, the distinct parts not yet invented. On Rider, there's no "headlight" verse and the final jam is a bit loose.

After High Time you can hear the opening Good Lovin' riff, but they settle on Easy Wind, one of the earliest versions (#7?). It has a long jam, including a Pigpen harp solo and Tom Constanten on the organ (you can hear them both, 6:15–6:25).

Casey Jones and Dire Wolf feature calliope organ sounds.

Link to recordings

1970 ST. LOUIS, MO

## KIEL OPERA HOUSE

The audience is treated to some interesting jams on this night, with "Tighten Up" amidst Dancin' In The Streets and the St. Stephen theme inside Good Lovin'.

The organ is prominent at the start of the Dancin' opener. Lesh goes high atop his bass (5:09–5:24), then starts a great tempo change around 6:30 picked up by the drums. This morphs into the two-chord "Tighten Up" jam. They stay on it about four minutes until a change of tempo and more high leads from Lesh.

Good Lovin' goes quickly from the first two verses into the drum solo (2:44–), then eventually resurfaces for the jam (10:19). This one really boils, Garcia and Lesh are both turbocharged. They catch a breath and start trading three-note lines, then Lesh is off to the races again.

They start a four-chord jam that sounds a bit like the occasionally played special break in Hard To Handle until Garcia begins to play with the St. Stephen theme (14:35–) (you can hear it clearly after the fifteen-minute mark). Then they begin to toss the Good Lovin' theme around like a Hacky Sack and return to the vocals.

We get a full St. Stephen later in the set, with more wonderful high notes from Lesh in the inside jam and ringing chords from Weir and/ or Garcia, a rocked-out ode to joy.

They finish big with an eighteen-minute Turn On Your Lovelight. Garcia pulls out his slide amidst Pigpen's rap backed by the "shine, on me" chorus (7:10–). It has a symphonic ending with a smashing of cymbals.

Link to recordings

1971 DETROIT, MI

# EASTOWN THEATER

Night two here, and it's another good one. Dark Star has a pretty, twinkling introduction; it quickly quiets and drifts into atonal off-kiltering (4:20–), then becomes sort of jazzy before we get the theme and verse one.

After ten minutes, they are racing again, Garcia briefly brandishing his chords (10:50–), then some fabulous jamming, which suddenly comes to a halt (12:58). The drums drop out from under them, like they were falling from a fifty-story building. It becomes a prelude to a funky but too brief "Feelin' Groovy" break, it's nearly over as fast as they start it.

Garcia invents a curious little theme (15:30–) and they go with it for a while, then pull off to the side of the road (17:30) before finding their way back to the main theme and verse two. The final notes fade off into the lonely tones of Me & Bobby McGee, Weir quick to pick up the vocal.

After a raging Cumberland Blues, with Lesh in full throat on harmony vocals, St. Stephen comes next carrying a low-tempo start. There would be just one more version (10/31/71) before a long hiatus.

The answer to The Answer Man is the same as it was three nights ago: Johnny B. Goode.

Other delights abound, including China Cat Sunflower and I Know You Rider. Hard to resist.

Link to recordings

## 1972 MILWAUKEE, WI

# PERFORMING ARTS CENTER

A long version of The Other One contains two treats inside: "Philo Stomp" and He's Gone.

The Other One slows as they get to the nine-minute mark and becomes a melodic Lesh solo with Bill's backing, referred to as "Philo Stomp" (see 10/18/72). Garcia joins, then Keith and Weir (great chords), and they jam without reference to The Other One. It soon sounds like a Weir-Garcia duet (12:40–),then Lesh returns to his "Stomp" theme.

After sixteen minutes, there's some electric piano and a sparse, new jam, the kind you might hear in Playing In The Band. Garcia shifts into higher gear (17:20–), later spasming weird and wobbly, wildly spinning out of control into sharp, jagged nothingness devoid of void. Other sounds include Weir's guitar strings on a chalkboard and Garcia's sobbing volume knob.

Rising out of these atonal ashes, Garcia calmly begins to play the opening lines of He's Gone. His inside solo is accompanied by some pretty lines from Keith and then Lesh's tumbling, descending bass notes. It's another beautifully rendered 1972 version.

There's an interesting end to the He's Gone exit jam as Lesh picks up his Other One bass line and Weir quickly goes to the lily fields verse. They end with a brief quote from Cryptical Envelopment.

"We got an equipment malfunction that we're gonna take care of, real quick, and uh, then we'll be right back with ya." –BW

They close it out with Casey Jones and Johnny B. Goode ("just like in the Fillmore movie!*" –BW).

Link to recordings

*Perhaps Weir was referring to *Fillmore*, a documentary film released on June 14, 1972 featuring the band's performances of Casey Jones and Johnny B. Goode on 7/2/71 (released on DVD, 2009).

## 1979 SPRINGFIELD, MA
# SPRINGFIELD CIVIC CENTER

After a seven-week respite, they start their Fall tour. Set two features five songs pre-Drums, nearly an hour of music. They finish the set with a Playing In The Band sandwich that wraps Drums, Space, and Wharf Rat. The performance is generally crisp, with some rusty vocals on a few tunes.

On the show-opening Promised Land, Garcia displays his melodic chops, wonderful phrases in the first solo and a well-crafted second, punctuated with a musical exclamation mark from Lesh to end it.

Scarlet Begonias starts set two. Garcia pulls out his lyrical paintbrush and carefully builds his inside solo. The first run is earnest, and on the second he's still taking his time articulating notes. A creative walk up the stairs into the third run thrills the crowd (the notes that spin out of it recall 2/3/79), then he makes another jaunty ascent into his fourth run.

The intro to Fire On The Mountain starts with a Garcia solo rather than the standard themes. Brent calls the peak with a surprising series of high-pitched notes. The first break has simple guitar lines that recite the main melody, the crowd loving it. At the end of the second break, Brent gets some space for a solo (8:43–9:14). We hear nifty fills from Weir during the third verse, then the grand descending theme and hurricane-speed guitar runs.

Playing In The Band starts with swishing cymbals from Bill and Mickey. The jam quiets after five minutes, then finds a compelling second wind with sheets of sound from Brent and Garcia stuttering on a note (8:24–). It resolves into a gentle kaleidoscope.

Wharf Rat's exit jam begins with some powerful drumming from Bill and Mickey and it launches Garcia into orbit. After the ten-minute mark, Garcia utters the Around And Around opening lick, but perhaps Weir shook him off as they quickly detour into a Playin'-style jam before a return to the Playing In The Band vocals.

Link to recordings

## 1990 HAMBURG, GERMANY
## SPORTHALLE HAMBURG

This is their fifth and final concert in Germany on this tour. An upbeat start to set two—Help → Slipknot! → Franklin's, then Truckin'—and an energetic finish.

Feel Like A Stranger opens set one. There are some good contributions by all players, but there's a rough transition out of a jam that feels a bit short.

The set closing Iko Iko has great Cajun accordion sounds; it's Hornsby's second rendition with the band (see 9/16/90). Garcia adds an effect and gives his guitar a horn flavor. Hornsby tacks on a grand piano statement towards the end, but they shut down the jam and head to intermission. Alas.

Set two: On He's Gone, they create a sonorous rendition of the "nothing's gonna bring him back" chorus. The vocals get the echo treatment, but there's no exit jam, just a fade to Drums.

During I Need A Miracle, the crowd does a nice job of filling in the final lyric on the choruses ("I need a miracle, every day"). The rocking tempo is carried over into The Wheel, an unusual transition first tried in 1988 (see 7/5/88). At this pace, the song swings like Touch Of Grey. There are some pretty lines from Garcia during the exit that call for further exploration, but they seem set on something higher tempo and make their way into Goin' Down The Road. Hornsby gets a verse and a slice of a solo that is low in the mix.

Around And Around brings the curtain down. It's the new-style version in which the midsection is a swaying, laid-back groove, rather than a step up in key that pushes the rock pedal to the metal.

Link to recordings

# OCTOBER 25

1969 San Francisco, CA, Winterland Ballroom

1973 Madison, WI, Dane County Coliseum

1979 New Haven, CT, Veterans Memorial Coliseum

1980 New York City, NY, Radio City Music Hall

1985 Pembroke Pines, FL, The Sportatorium

1989 Miami, FL, Miami Arena

1969 SAN FRANCISCO, CA

## WINTERLAND BALLROOM

We have recordings of Dark Star → St. Stephen → The Eleven → Turn On Your Lovelight and some of High Time (Deadbase lists five other songs that preceded those). Stephen Stills appears on Lovelight.

A fine Dark Star, with whimsical keyboard runs from Tom Constanten before the introductory jam dissolves. Garcia picks up the main theme again and it gets a jazzier suit, then reverts to its normal self before the first verse comes around 7:02.

There's some slashing and bashing from Lesh and the drummers before it quiets for a spell. They begin to play loosely with the "Feelin' Groovy" theme, Lesh carrying the melody (12:35–), Weir picking up the chords. Later, Weir and Garcia start the two-chord Tighten Up jam. The peak around nineteen minutes is unique, then Garcia latches on to the main Dark Star theme and they wind down for the second verse.

St. Stephen features huge blasts of bass from Lesh following the "one man gathers" lyric. There's more of his powerful, percussive playing on The Eleven. At the end of the vocals, we get a brief interlude of drums-only (7:01–), then Lesh leads as Garcia drops out for awhile.

Stills joins the "let it shine" chorus on Turn On Your Lovelight (6:24–). Later, you can hear more of his guitar work (it's loud, but not particularly interesting).

"May be a little prejudiced but let's get, we should get one thing straight, on any given night, the very greatest rock 'n' roll band in the world, The Grateful Dead, please." –BG

Link to recordings

1973 MADISON, WI

# DANE COUNTY COLISEUM

This evening features a Dark Star with a Mind Left Body Jam inside, but the most compelling jam arguably occurs in Eyes Of The World.

A lazy, hazy start to Dark Star, the main theme winks and disappears. After a good five-minute soak in the floatation tank, we hear a lighter, fluffier version of the Mind Left Body Jam. It's over rather quickly.

The Dark Star jam picks up in speed and intensity around the nine-minute mark and that, too, fades. A minute later, Garcia revives the main theme and we get verse one (13:12), sung in a near whisper as if coming from beyond the grave.

There's a brief trio segment (Weir-Lesh-Bill) then feedback and shimmers, lonely notes calling for their mates. Garcia's guitar begins to speak in tongues, solitude giving way to confusion, a multitudinous babble of bent, demented sounds that spin into a sucking, swirling whirlpool of weird. Feeling banished for eternity beyond the Seventh Circle of sound, suddenly a lifeline appears: the happy, life-giving bounce of Eyes Of The World.

After Lesh's bass solo (7:04–8:23), this version features one of the better back halves of Eyes, with sustained, powerful jamming. In a couple of places, Keith and Garcia's licks might remind you of Take Five. Towards the end, they drop a thousand feet in ten seconds and enter Stella Blue light as a feather.

Set one has a fine jam in Playing In The Band, straight-ahead improv until the eleven-minute mark when things turn slightly dissonant.

Link to recordings

1979 NEW HAVEN, CT

## VETERANS MEMORIAL COLISEUM

Don't let the Don't Ease Me In opener fool you. Go to set two. Go directly to set two.

Shakedown Street shines. The exit jam is reborn with three minutes to go, a thrilling breakout. Garcia pushes it through the roof, among the most exciting versions you'll hear.

Passenger's next, and on the second break Garcia goes hypersonic, a torrent of notes delivered at Terrapin Transit speed. Listen to the soundboard for the full effect.

Estimated Prophet has a couple of stirring peaks during the inside solo. The exit jam is led by Brent, a solo on his twirling toy piano. Thereafter, Garcia is again in overdrive, a rush of bubbly notes.

After Eyes Of The World, we get at least five minutes of Space before Drums (including bass bonking, guitar gargling, fountaining fireworks, daffy duck, cats meowing, swooping synth, drum rolls, and a siren).

Link to recordings

1980 NEW YORK CITY, NY

## RADIO CITY MUSIC HALL

Lots and lots and lots of Grateful Dead. Ten songs in the opening acoustic set. Nine more in the first electric set, and nine in the second, plus the encore.

The first set has some rarities. El Paso is just their third acoustic version since Fall 1970 (Weir plays it acoustic again during their final years, starting with 9/30/93). Heaven Help The Fool makes an appearance, only played live this Fall.

The electric numbers tonight unmistakably sound like truncated versions. For example: the set-opening Mississippi Half Step finds Garcia squeezing juicy notes between the verses, but there's just a short inside solo after that, paired with a similarly short outro jam.

Set three, Saint Of Circumstance, the "rain falling down" jam begins with heavy feedback from Garcia. A big build, though short, they nail the landing.

Uncle John's Band → Playing In The Band before Drums features an interesting transition between the two. The guitars start up the Playin' intro while the drummers are still finishing the UJB jam.

The Playing In The Band jam begins quietly, understated, spacious, then develops a percolating undercurrent and grows slowly in intensity. Around 7:45, the guitars seem to drop out, leaving Brent and the drummers to lead a trio, a special two-minute segment.

Out of Space, The Other One would nearly fit on a three-minute single; we only get the first verse before Black Peter. The rock 'n' roll finish— Around And Around → One More Saturday Night—has Weir's youthful energy and some fine solos from Brent.

Link to recordings

## 1985 PEMBROKE PINES, FL

# THE SPORTATORIUM

The start of the Fall tour unveils a couple of rare set openers: Deal begins set one, Morning Dew starts set two.

Likely a surprising, exciting start for fans, Deal opened the concert for just the third time (9/30/72 and 5/18/77). They would never do it again.

The inside Deal solo has a Day Job flavor, Garcia's in decent voice relative to the year. Amidst the outro jam, you can hear Bill and Mickey turn up the heat with half a dozen strokes (5:12–) and the crowd responds.

They close the set with Let It Grow, Garcia in high-speed mode. The jam begins with crunchy bass bombs from Lesh. A high-tempo, complex jam fills an exciting, well-played version.

Morning Dew begins set two without ado. Garcia starts it off with a single chord and away they go. A more frequent set opener than Deal historically, it had started a final frame just once since 1973 (see 6/14/85, and 7/12/87). The final jam has a good midsection, stretched out with long runs and creative phrasing. Weir is the first to begin the grand chord sweeping (9:45), then Garcia swoops in with his own trills.

On Eyes Of The World, Garcia starts with a tempo he's hard pressed to maintain, yet he somehow pulls it off. Around 1:45, Weir seems game and turns up the heat. To get a sense of the torrid pace, check out the "redeemer" verse ("fades away" becomes one word).

Link to recordings

1989 MIAMI, FL

## MIAMI ARENA

Playing In The Band opens set two and stretches over sixteen minutes, not including the Uncle John's Band in the middle.

There's some delicious drumming from Bill and Mickey between the initial Playing In The Band verses. The jam begins with Garcia tracing a melodic line, Lesh carving his own underneath. Lead guitar effects are turned on, off, and back on, eventually getting around to the flute. There are shimmering dronescapes (9:59–), high-speed runs, and then wonderful descending chords from Brent. They bottom it out until Garcia picks up Uncle John's Band, introducing the clean, stirring lines of the familiar melody.

The harmony vocals are a bit rough around the edges on this one, and later Weir and Garcia are singing different words ("how does the song go?" indeed). This version is kind of saved by the exit jam (8:00–), though Garcia is slow out of the gate. Brent is the one who sounds spry but he isn't front and center.

After the final vocals, it's back into the D minor jam for a minute, Garcia's trumpet effect engages and he begins to toy with the Playin' theme. They continue jamming, Brent trying to take it chromatic if not dissonant before Garcia insists on a return to the Playin' vocals. It's a rough re-entry, though Brent reels off a great repeating figure, Baba O'Riley-like to end it. Garcia begins to strum Standing On The Moon (#13) before they've capped it off and that's where they go.

Truckin' is next. During the jam, Garcia gets into an Other One pattern, but it dissolves quickly. He then seems to drop out, leaving an interesting quintet jam in his wake, Weir and Brent leading. They yield to Drums.

Link to recordings

# OCTOBER 26

1966 San Francisco, CA, The North Face Ski Shop
   (no setlist, no recording)

1969 San Francisco, CA, Winterland Ballroom

1971 Rochester, NY, University of Rochester, The Palestra

1972 Cincinnati, OH, Music Hall

1980 New York City, NY, Radio City Music Hall

1985 Tampa, FL, University of South Florida, Sun Dome

1989 Miami, FL, Miami Arena

1969 SAN FRANCISCO, CA

## WINTERLAND BALLROOM

We have seven songs from a setlist of thirteen, plus the opening Instrumental.

The opener is laid back and lilting like Octopus's Garden, which was released by The Beatles on 9/26/69 (this piece has the same chords, but they're in the key of C instead of E that the Fab Four use).

Hard To Handle is one of at least three Pigpen tunes tonight, including an early version of Next Time You See Me, as well as a ten-minute version of Easy Wind that features a gloriously grungy solo from Weir (4:45–) then soaring lines from Garcia (6:40–) (see also 9/20/70).

Link to recordings


1971 ROCHESTER, NY

## UNIVERSITY OF ROCHESTER, THE PALESTRA

The big numbers are at the end of set two: lengthy versions of Truckin' and The Other One, with a seamless segue into Johnny B. Goode to close.

The first set is a superbloom of sixteen songs. After the opening Bertha, they explain Pigpen's absence and Keith's presence. El Paso is a bright spot, Garcia's guitar a chatterbox, spilling over with cheerful, creative fills and phrases. On the set-closing One More Saturday Night (#6), Weir ad-libs some lyrics to the last verse: "I may be young and crazy but I don't can't see reason one; for fightin' or complainin' when we should be havin' fun."

Truckin' has a rollicking, hard-rocking final jam. It quiets and sounds like they will return to the vocal chorus (7:30), but they press on. Garcia starts to make Other One sounds (8:25) yet it's still a Truckin' jam. A minute later, the metamorphosis is complete, but they detour into Drums.

The Other One comes next, a sixteen-minute sojourn of rage and reflection. After the "trembled and exploded" line, we hear a head-splitting fill from Garcia. The jam quiets a bit after four minutes, then roars back to life (6:10), Weir slashing hard and cutting a path through the musical overgrowth.

By 7:30, Garcia has taken them over an atonal cliff. After seemingly finding their footing and putting the bus back on terra firma, they detour into another shrieking cul de sac of ghoulish sounds.

Eleven minutes in, they're back on the main road, quietly teasing the main theme. There's a final quiet patch before cymbals crash (13:35), Lesh blasts (13:50), and the bus revs its engine heading to verse two, including a wonderful rising chord pattern from Weir.

Johnny B. Goode has the same savage energy as the one rendered at the closing of the Fillmore West (7/2/71).

"Thanks a lot everybody we'll see ya'll later." –JG

Link to recordings

## MUSIC HALL

Tonight's highlights include a Playing In The Band that runs nearly thirty minutes, and a twenty-minute, one-verse Dark Star.

Set two begins with a forceful, straight-ahead version of Playing In The Band, a clinic on Bill's drumming. There are only brief flirtations with strangeness in the first ten minutes. After twelve minutes, it begins to slow and quiet, musical sails luffing.

Later, the jam becomes a bass and drums duo (17:25–20:14). Lesh then begins a new melodic line, the rest of the band joins and they're off to the races, leading to Garcia's wild, weird, and watery lines.

Around the twenty-four-minute mark, Garcia begins to play with the main theme and they make their way back to the vocals.

After three more songs, Truckin' is given a low-key treatment. They simply saunter until the jam begins and Garcia slides into power chords, then he takes flight. There's a quick segue into the Nobody's Fault But Mine theme. They wind it all the way down (2:45) until Bill's soft drum rolls take them into Dark Star.

Dreamy and wandering, they take a casual stroll through the cosmos. The music goes through a pretty place (7:25) then builds to their first crescendo. Over that hill, we take a walk through a strange valley (9:25–) with no vocals on the horizon.

There's a neat little pattern from Weir (11:40–), some fast licks from Garcia, and these, too, disappear.

It's Lesh who finally picks up the main theme, quiet as a mouse (14:12–). Garcia takes the baton and we get the first Dark Star verse (15:24). The rest of the way remains largely an inconspicuous tiptoe through the infinite. Keith and Bill play a duet (18:35–19:25) that dissolves into drumming. Where shall they go?

Garcia finds himself alone in the spotlight, playing guitar lines that could take them anywhere. But after Weir begins the Sugar Magnolia chords, that's where they ride.

Link to recordings

## 1980 NEW YORK CITY, NY
# RADIO CITY MUSIC HALL

"Billy has a broken drum, and ya can't beat that." –BW

The concert starts with a fine acoustic set. Brent shines with solos on the opening Iko Iko as well as on the next one, Dark Hollow. A beautiful It Must Have Been The Roses follows. Garcia sings "one pane of glass in the window" as soft and low as he can go, accompanied by Weir's single harmonic, Bill and Mickey's gentle brushing of the drums, and Brent's handful of careful notes.

"On The Road Again?" –BW

After consulting his colleagues, Weir launches their take on a traditional tune they played consistently on the Warfield and Radio City stands (see also 12/1/66) (originally recorded around 1929 by The Memphis Jug Band).

In set three, Estimated Prophet builds to a nice peak after the ten-minute mark, a highlight. The drummers start rolling and there's a hint that Eyes Of The World might be coming, but they slow it all the way down and begin He's Gone.

Here we find strong singing from Garcia, the crowd claps along during the "nothing's gonna bring him back" chorus. The exit jam is different and short-lived. They quickly change it up (11:00–) and are going gosh knows where.

Link to recordings


1985 TAMPA, FL

## UNIVERSITY OF SOUTH FLORIDA, SUN DOME

After a 259-mile journey through the Everglades, the band arrives here for the second night of the tour.

Gimme Some Lovin' opens, a great spot for it ("so glad you made it"). But it's kind of downhill from there for set one.

Greatest Story follows and sounds sluggish. Weir seems to miss his cue for the "Abraham and Isaac" lines and the jam gets off to a slow start. Dupree's Diamond Blues bats third; it's Garcia's first vocal of the night and his voice is on the ropes. It's still ultra-gruff through Stagger Lee, but his other songs present fewer challenges (Big Railroad Blues, and Don't Ease Me In, which closes the set).

Set two fares better. China Cat Sunflower starts it off, and Bill and Mickey give the transition jam a swift kick in the rear, helping Garcia drive it to a rousing peak. I Know You Rider is lively; they stretch out the initial jam. Garcia takes three runs before Weir's "sun will shine" verse. As he starts to sing his "headlight" verse, Weir throws in his China Cat licks. A highlight.

Throwing Stones has spirited soloing on the inside jam, and massive Lesh bombs at the end of it. Weir savages the "rich man in his summer home" line. The song has a strange exit, Weir and then Brent begin singing Goin' Down The Road before anyone is playing the song. But they get it cranked up quickly.

Encore: In The Midnight Hour (fourth of seven this year, the most since 1970).

Link to recordings

## 1989 MIAMI, FL
# MIAMI ARENA

The last night of the Fall mini-tour, a parting gift is the twenty-six-minute Dark Star, nearly half of it a deep Space exploration.

Set two: we hear almost two minutes of shimmering cymbals, feedback, and electronic piano before Garcia sounds the opening notes of Dark Star. After the first verse (2:10), his voice notably scraggly, he quickly goes to echoey effects. Later, there's some picking on an old sub-theme (5:40) briefly recalling 1969.

After ten minutes, we get a Mr. Kite psychedelia carousel ride (10:40). They pick up the main melody after thirteen minutes (Weir finds it first) and we get verse two (13:59). Garcia's voice is scruffy to hoarse, and he has some trouble navigating these simple lyrics.

They quickly disappear into chimes and assorted sounds, it's all Space for the next twelve minutes, no jamming. Drums is next, then a Space that begins with ghostly voices.

The Stella Blue exit jam carries some of the same echoey electronica.

Encore: We Bid You Goodnight, their sixth and last for the year (the most since 1970).

Deadbase X respondents ranked this tied for third best of the year. Headyversion voters named this Dark Star eleventh best *all-time* (ahead of 12/6/73, 10/18/74, and 3/29/90, among many others).

Link to recordings

# OCTOBER 27

1971 Syracuse, NY, Onondaga War Memorial Auditorium

1972 Columbus, OH, Veterans Memorial Auditorium

1973 Indianapolis, IN, State Fair Coliseum

1979 South Yarmouth, MA, Cape Cod Coliseum

1980 New York City, NY, Radio City Music Hall

1984 Berkeley, CA, Berkeley Community Theater

1990 Paris, France, The Zenith

1991 Oakland, CA, Oakland Coliseum Arena

## 1971 SYRACUSE, NY

# ONONDAGA WAR MEMORIAL AUDITORIUM

"For the benefit of all you folks out in radioland we are The Grateful Dead." –PL

That's their lead-in to the opening Casey Jones, a quintessential starter this year. Weir decides to introduce their second number: "…a little song about wanton death and destruction…called Me and My Uncle."

Jack Straw (#5) bats fourth, Garcia explodes with a surprisingly exciting fill after the "die is shaking" line. On the final break, still in its infancy, listen for Keith's jangling piano and another interesting guitar fill after "by the morning light."

Tennessee Jed (#6) is played high tempo, normal for this time frame, nearly as rocking as the next number, Beat It On Down The Line. Garcia is fast and fluid there as well.

Set two: the Truckin' jam is a foot-stomping barnburner with searing lead guitar lines amidst the final sung chorus.

Not Fade Away features more great soloing from Garcia. It subsides into a drum solo, ending with Bill's Not Fade Away cadence that yields to a Jam. It's unclear what makes this a "China Cat Jam," except for Weir playing his China Cat licks three minutes in. Also of note: a stirring string of pull offs from Garcia towards the end of the first minute. After Weir's bit of sorcery, they enter Goin' Down The Road.

The final minute has the traditional two-chord coda from this era, then it's back to Not Fade Away to close. Garcia's guitar answers Weir's "love is love not fade away," perhaps filling in for Pigpen's missing voice (his return is still a ways off, 12/1/71).

Link to recordings

## 1972 COLUMBUS, OH

# VETERANS MEMORIAL AUDITORIUM

A big set two: Truckin' → The Other One → Mississippi Half Step, plus Morning Dew and a double encore.

At the end of the Truckin' jam, the crowd keeps clapping in time as the band figures out what they want to do. It's not quite a Nobody's Fault jam, but plenty low-down and funky. Bill tosses it up into the air and it seems like anybody's choice.

They continue the bluesy jam for the first three minutes of The Other One track, then it begins to shapeshift into something jazzier. By the five-minute mark, the metamorphosis is complete, a surreptitious slide into The Other One.

After the Spanish lady comes to Weir, they take it down to a simmer, and a brief Lesh solo emerges amidst Bill's quiet rolls. It's an interesting journey from there, with jazzy improvisations, another quiet wandering. What's next?

It's a nifty segue into Mississippi Half Step, the only time they tried this (see also the Dark Star → Half Step unicorn, 10/23/72).

They continue to inspire, following with Morning Dew. It's beautifully rendered, with care and sensitivity, pathos and passion.

Encore: Uncle John's Band and One More Saturday Night.

Link to recordings

## 1973 INDIANAPOLIS, IN
## STATE FAIR COLISEUM

This is an underrated performance, likely due to the quality of the recordings. Dive in anyway. The performance is crisp, inventive, and inspiring, start to finish.

Set two sparkles. Me & My Uncle is a snappy opener; you'll think you walked into an 1880s western saloon. Weir is feeling feisty: "grabbed a bottle, cracked him in the jaw."

Mid-set, the main meal is a double-decker Playing In The Band sandwich, with Mississippi Half Step and Big River inside. The jam begins in quiet contemplation, Bill has the tempo on simmer. After seven minutes, Garcia throws in a Slipknot!-like descending line. A couple minutes later, there's an interesting dissonant passage in which they drag a musical line through the avant-garde mud.

After coming down from the jam's peak, for reasons unknown, they slip into Mississippi Half Step. A good 1973 rendition, there are a couple of beats of silence before they then launch a raging Big River, Garcia's guitar full of fury.

They close the curtain on that one, and the very next beat finds Weir wandering. It could be anything, though Garcia's underwatery tone soon suggests a return to Playing In The Band.

Other delights:

* Truckin', with Keith's strong Hammond B3 midway through, and Garcia's guitar gunfire during the jam

* The Nobody's Fault But Mine jam. Keith takes the lead on it (2:15–4:02) until Garcia returns with his slide. The final

minute sounds like it could launch into The Other One,
but they go somewhere else

* A couple of Garcia ballads that follow back-to-back:
  Wharf Rat and Stella Blue, with an interesting transition
  between the two.

They finish with a monumental Sugar Magnolia. Garcia delivers a stirring
solo on the final break; it sounds like they'll never run out of steam.

More? Try the set one closer, China Cat Sunflower Dark Star I Know
You Rider for Weir's brilliant lead lines in the transition jam, Garcia
taking it up another level then launching the "Feelin' Groovy" theme,
then a quick pivot into I Know You Rider with more peak moments
there.

In a year filled with great performances, this one deserves more
recognition.

Link to recordings

 **1979 SOUTH YARMOUTH, MA**
## CAPE COD COLISEUM

Set two is loaded with inventive jamming. The major highlight is the
opening Dancin' In The Streets into Franklin's Tower.

Dancin' has a particularly funky-disco feel to it, Brent's Prophet-5 synthesizer a prime co-conspirator. The Jam turns for home in a unique way
(10:33–), Garcia dancing chords down the fretboard like a ballroom
dancer, Lesh racing him to the bottom.

Franklin's Tower has two sublime breaks. After the "pleasure tends" verse, Garcia delicately steps up the stairs to a heavenly peak (9:00–), Bill and Mickey stir up the seas behind him, and Weir's soft triplets come on their heels.

The final jam after the "four winds" verse quiets, intricate and lovely. Is there anything left? They're softly percolating and then hatch something new: Brent's swinging licks; Lesh's three-point punctuation marks; Brent's chords; and the Swiss watch comes back to life! Garcia trills his chords, Weir unleashes a set of ringing triplets, then Bill and Mickey come galloping out of the stables. Brilliant.

He's Gone → The Other One is next, twenty-five minutes loaded with jamming, including a brief section near the end of He's Gone that remind some of a high-speed Caution Jam. The Other One starts with a ferocious rumble from Lesh. They construct a huge crescendo, including more Lesh histrionics courtesy of his crunchy sledgehammer. There's more wild jamming after verse two. Great.

An inspired performance, Deadbase X respondents ranked it best of the year by a wide margin (in the Deadbase V survey, it trailed 12/1/79 by a few votes. The versions of Dancin' and Franklin's are each in the all-time top ten of Headyversion voters).

Link to recordings

## RADIO CITY MUSIC HALL

There's a unique opener to set three—Truckin' → Scarlet Begonias → Fire On The Mountain—and a rousing close: I Need A Miracle → Bertha → Johnny B. Goode.

The acoustic set opens with The Race Is On, only the second time it would ever open a concert (5/1/70). Weir, clearly enthused, ends it with a, "Hey, now!" ("thank you, thank you"). The now usual wooden delights follow.

Set two ends with Deal, which features an inspired inside solo from Garcia, and we get the new three-chord exit jam, still a youngster (see 9/25/80).

Truckin' begins the final set; one wonders what the crowd was expecting as the jam wound down. Perhaps they imagined one of the usual blues-oriented suspects like I Need A Miracle (you can hear Weir's slide) or a ballad such as He's Gone. And then, in the strangest of places, Garcia picks out the first notes of Scarlet Begonias.

The heart-of-gold-band-jam has a little Latin motif around the seven-minute mark. On the final Fire On The Mountain break, Garcia shows flashes of speed before a quiet unraveling into Drums.

Bertha is the only one of its kind performed on the Radio City stand (they did one at the Warfield, 10/2/80). Garcia and the drummers are on the mark here, a fine version.

Encore: Casey Jones (one of four played on the Warfield-Radio City tour).

Link to recordings

1984 BERKELEY, CA

## BERKELEY COMMUNITY THEATER

A week after the end of their East Coast tour, they begin the first of six nights here.

Set two has six songs before Drums. He's Gone gets the fourth slot, and they transition easily into Wang Dang Doodle from there, a Willie Dixon song performed for just the second time this year (the next one won't come until 3/27/86).

When it's done, they seem unsure about whether to do another tune, drifting into wandering guitar picking and assorted sounds like you might hear in Space. Bill and Mickey then begin the cadence for Brent's I Don't Need Love.

Near the end of the set, they have some trouble starting Goin' Down The Road; Garcia plays at a speedy tempo that the other guys have trouble latching onto.

During the One More Saturday Night finale, Weir lets out a big blow on his whistle amidst the final chorus (4:03). Apparently, Lesh then removed the offending, tiny woodwind instrument, as Weir asks for the crowd's help in getting it back before the encore.

"So on the count of three, everybody say, 'Hey, Phil, give him back his whistle.'"

Some good playing here and there, but Deadbase respondents give far higher marks to other nights on this stand (11/2/84, 11/3/84, 10/31/84).

Link to recordings

1990 PARIS, FRANCE
## THE ZENITH

After two days off, the band plays their first concert in Paris since 1981. Saint Of Circumstance returns to the repertoire (see 6/18/89) and becomes a mainstay once again. A full Playing In The Band is split by Drums and Space.

Set one has a fairly standard opening (Bucket → Sugaree → Minglewood) and closing (Masterpiece → Bird Song → Promised Land), but mid-set there's a Black Throated Wind, their fifth since the revival earlier in the year. Hornsby's piano adds a nice touch on Minglewood and Promised Land.

Set two: they begin Saint Of Circumstance from a cold start, and the jam sounds a bit stiff. The following Crazy Fingers fizzles out around 8:40. They wander around until giving Weir room to begin Playing In The Band.

Stella Blue has a particularly energetic, articulate inside solo from Garcia, perhaps his best stretch of the night (his final run on Promised Land to close set one is also good, see the video). The Stella outro jam is short, not much development.

Not Fade Away is just five minutes; the rest of it is a fading vocal chorus until the crowd takes over (7:10–).

Link to recordings

1991 OAKLAND, CA

## OAKLAND COLISEUM ARENA

After a month off, the first of four here.

Coming two days after the tragic death of Bill Graham, their long-time friend and concert promoter, the performance becomes a moving tribute.

Surprises include a Sugar Magnolia opener, and guest appearances by Carlos Santana and Gary Duncan of Quicksilver Messenger Service on Iko Iko and Mona.

Sugar Magnolia rarely opened a set, let alone a concert, and most times only on New Year's Eve. That night was Bill Graham's domain, and this show's opener was likely a tribute to him (it was his favorite song, according to many sources).

Garcia's inside solo on Sugar Magnolia nails the emotionally poignant notes, and Hornsby steps up midway through. They segue into Sugaree, leaving Sunshine Daydream for another day (see 11/3/91 for this missing piece).

Touch Of Grey closes set one, a particularly reassuring song under the circumstances of Graham's passing (it closed the first frame just twice since 1984: 3/27/89 and 7/4/86).

In set two, Iko Iko and Mona (the latter last played on 3/25/72) turn into a twenty-seven-minute jam session. Duncan has the first Iko solo (4:00–), Santana is next, and then Garcia is thrown into the mix with his MIDI engaged. The song takes on a true New Orleans flavor around the seven-minute mark.

At the end of Iko, Bill and Mickey start a Not Fade Away-style beat. Garcia seems to be singing "Hey, Bo Diddley," but Weir takes over and sings the first line of Mona. Duncan has the first solo, rocking it hard.

As they near the five-minute mark, the tune begins to head into Supplication territory, transitioning from classic rock to fusion. After eight minutes, it starts to feel a bit like a Slipknot! jam. Later, it becomes avant-garde/spacey (more effects from Garcia) and seems headed to points unknown (12:30–). Bill and Mickey finally pick up the backbeat (14:30) for one last romp over the Mona rhythm before they head to Drums.

Not your average guest artist jam session.

Encore: Knockin' On Heaven's Door.

Link to recordings

# OCTOBER 28

1966 Davis, CA, University of California, Davis, Freeborn Hall (no setlist, no recording)

1972 Cleveland, OH, Public Hall

1977 Kansas City, KS, Soldiers & Sailors Memorial Hall

1979 South Yarmouth, MA, Cape Cod Coliseum

1984 Berkeley, CA, Berkeley Community Theater

1985 Atlanta, GA, Fox Theater

1990 Paris, France, The Zenith

1991 Oakland, CA, Oakland Coliseum Arena

## 1972 CLEVELAND, OH
# PUBLIC HALL

Tonight's highlights include another big Dark Star into Sugar Magnolia, their first Candyman in a year, and one of only two 1972 performances of Attics Of My Life (you won't hear another one until 10/9/89).

Dark Star begins with long swan dives emanating from Garcia's volume knob, a lush, languorous beginning. After five minutes, there's a big change of direction; Bill's drums and Keith's piano lead the turn, then it's Garcia's stuttering guitar gathering speed.

They make another push after 7:30, Lesh and Bill driving. Garcia does a final stair stepping to the top, then re-touches the main Dark Star melody (9:31–). They wander quietly until another rendezvous with the theme, all hands now on deck for the first verse (11:28).

After some of Garcia's underwatery tone, they edge toward full-on Space (14:40); it's full of feedback and Bill's drums. Lesh starts what is called "Philo Stomp" (16:54) (see also 10/24/72). Bill steps on the gas (17:25) before the other guys join, and Garcia unloads a shrieking warbler (19:30–).

They move on from Lesh's dream to jazzier climes, then back to Space, largely Garcia's atonal, weird wanderings and Bill's free drumming, winding it up higher and higher, creating musical G forces that could render some listeners unconscious. When all hope of harmony seems lost, we hear Bill's lone tom-tom and suddenly, Weir's lifesaving Sugar Magnolia licks.

Set one offers yet another adventure, a twenty-two-minute Playing In The Band to close the first half. Throughout the concert, Bill's drumming is up in the mix, a front row seat from which to observe his work.

Link to recordings

## 1977 KANSAS CITY, KS

# SOLDIERS & SAILORS MEMORIAL HALL

After a twelve-day break, the band moves north into the heartland, their first visit to Kansas in five years (11/13/72).

The best performances here seem to come during the "smaller" songs. In set one, there's a tight, long Supplication jam. Set two, on the Samson & Delilah opener, Garcia's first solo is full of fire, and the end of his second also rages. During Passenger, everything sounds in sync, the drum patterns perfectly matched to the tune, a fine slide solo from Garcia with two runs, and a crisp segue back to the vocals (no second solo).

He's Gone is more elongated than epic; the exit jam (11:53–) goes five minutes before devolving into percussion. There is a nice rebuild reaching a peak around the sixteen-minute mark.

After Drums, there are some timing issues with the vocal entrances in most of the songs. On Not Fade Away, the main jam goes from plodding to nap-time. After ten minutes, it disappears into lead guitar whistles and tambourine shakes. It's a very different performance of the song compared to other versions this month (e.g., 10/11/77, 10/15/77, 10/29/77).

After a slow-as-molasses Stella Blue, they try their first Goin' Down The
Road in a month. They vamp on Garcia's intro line for a full minute,
then the drumming patterns keep shifting throughout the song. The
final break sounds slapdash, though Garcia's last two runs are exciting.
There's no traditional two-chord coda; they go straight into Around
And Around.

Encore: the recently revived Casey Jones. This, too, feels a bit off-kilter,
although perhaps appropriate for a tale of toot and trainwrecks.

Link to recordings

## 1979 SOUTH YARMOUTH, MA
## CAPE COD COLISEUM

Another great night here. The set two opening China Cat Sunflower →
I Know You Rider is the standout.

A wonderful example of their Swiss watch at work, the transition jam
between China Cat and Rider sparkles. Around 5:30, Garcia goes into
whirling dervish mode, then blasts out into new country. He soon starts
to center around a small figure and it sounds like they are ready to head
into I Know You Rider. But no! Garcia spins away, and the jam continues.

They hit the seven-minute mark and seem ready to enter Rider, all cen-
tered on the D chord in their own way. But Garcia once again spins a
new web, and they each scatter like mice fleeing a ravenous cat.

Weir starts his "sun will shine" verse singing Garcia's "I wish I was a
headlight" line. He makes up for it by tossing in a beautiful three-chord
descending lick. Rather than going straight to the next verse as in later

years, Garcia gets a solo and he hits it out of the park, two fabulous runs punctuated powerfully by the rest of the band.

The final break is a tidal wave, with a thunderous trilled run from Garcia into the F chord. Then all hell breaks loose, Lesh blowing the building to kingdom come.

And that's just the start of the second set.

Drums is not to be missed. Bill and Mickey thrash the daylights out of the kettle drums, bringing their lines together at the end to a single, deafening conclusion (on the soundboard, you can hear one of them counting down to the final beat).

Nearly an hour of music pre-Drums, they close with just two songs, but both shine. Stella Blue features heartbreaking guitar lines on the outro section. Sugar Magnolia features a great jam and a brilliant finish.

Long overshadowed by the first night here, this performance has ascended into Deadbase respondents' top five for the year (in the Deadbase V survey, it was outside the top fifteen).

Link to recordings

## 1984 BERKELEY, CA
# BERKELEY COMMUNITY THEATER

The second night of this stand, there are just six songs in set two but plenty of jamming. The opening Terrapin → Playing In The Band → China Doll → Drums is a highlight.

In set one, you can hear the intimacy of this small venue at the start of C.C. Rider. Before that one—Althea—Garcia sketches plenty of mercurial, serpentine lines, ranging far and wide on the fretboard.

Set two: on China Doll, the inside solo has a heavy echoey effect a la Hell In A Bucket, two runs. Brent's delicate harpsichord chimes shimmer throughout. After the final vocal line, six dreamy runs, who knows what's next.

Garcia revisits Playing In The Band and they jam on for another ten minutes. Down to a whispery guitar line around the six-minute mark, assorted sounds then creep in from the shadows.

They yield the floor to Bill and Mickey, more percussion than drumming; there are sounds from a South American rainforest, with a persistent melodic line. Space finds Garcia loosely quoting Bach (5:34–) and concocting a sweet segue into The Wheel.

Link to recordings

## 1985 ATLANTA, GA
# FOX THEATER

An interesting opening to the concert: Sugaree gets the pole position for the third time in five years (they would not do this again). Then they launch their first performance of Kansas City, a Leiber-Stoller composition from the '50s.

"I wonder how many of you were watchin' TV last night? Here we go." –BW

That's Weir's intro to the jump blues number, likely a reference to the Kansas City Royals winning Game Seven of the World Series the night before. Brent takes a solo on the Fender Rhodes, then Weir launches his slide. They'd try this song once more (11/5/85).

Set two opens with their seventh Scarlet Begonias → Touch Of Grey coupling (there would be another, 3/25/86). As they transition to the "we will survive" chorus, the crowd goes wild, apparently at the sight of the unfurling of a banner behind the stage. Weir moves straight into Women Are Smarter and waits for the rhythm section to kick in.

The jams tonight sound short, like CliffsNotes versions. On Women Are Smarter, Garcia's first solo seems to end early, then he putters while we wait for Weir to sing the next verse. In the Truckin' jam, after the peak, there are just four runs before entering Smokestack Lightning. The Stella Blue exit jam lasts less than a minute.

Not to worry, check out the next night here.

Link to recordings

## 1990 PARIS, FRANCE
# THE ZENITH

The band closes set one with one of Hornsby's tunes, Stander On The Mountain; they'll do two more of those this Fall.

Victim Or The Crime opens set two. In the final minute, the spacey growling drone gives way to a new jam that finds Garcia in a happier mode, while Weir remains in discordant contradiction. Out of this spacey stew comes the salsa-like, swinging chords of Eyes Of The World.

Arguably, in the post-Brent era, Drums → Space increasingly becomes the most interesting aspect of Grateful Dead concerts. To wit, after four minutes of Drums, we get the sounds of barnyard animals—yes, send in the cows—along with a psychologically disturbed rainforest bird. A melodic line develops, supported by percussion. The cows return, the bird squawks, frogs croak, and a tugboat emits foghorns in the distance. Ribbit.

Set one is long, ten songs and over seventy minutes of music. Touch Of Grey opens and the new, layered keyboard/piano arrangement seems to work here, Lesh crunching away underneath.

Link to recordings

### 1991 OAKLAND, CA

## OAKLAND COLISEUM

Second of four on this stand, the set two Playing In The Band has an interesting jam at the end.

Playin' is the third of three songs pre-Drums. Between the first chorus and next verse, Hornsby delivers some particularly percussive piano licks. He seems to be chomping at the bit, ready to race into the jam.

After eleven minutes, they leave the Playin' theme behind and race through an elsewhere landscape, some of their best work of the night.

There are great piano lines in Stella Blue, like Hornsby's reply to Garcia's "down every lonely street" line, a classic blues statement. Then Garcia powerfully delivers the next verse—"I've stayed in every blue light, cheap hotel"—with rising piano notes in its wake. The band really hits the note here, a good example of a peak 1991 moment. The exit jam exudes achingly beautiful sounds.

Link to recordings

# OCTOBER 29

1968 San Francisco, CA, The Matrix
(Mickey and the Heartbeats) (no setlist, no recording)

1971 Cleveland, OH, Allen Theater

1973 St. Louis, MO, Kiel Auditorium

1977 Dekalb, IL, Northern Illinois University (NIU),
Chick Evans Field House

1980 New York City, NY, Radio City Music Hall

1985 Atlanta, GA, Fox Theater

1971 CLEVELAND, OH

## ALLEN THEATER

A Friday night gig at a fifty-year-old downtown theater. The performance highlight is the thirty-seven-minute That's It For The Other One with a Me & My Uncle middle.

Cryptical Envelopment leads quickly to six minutes of drum soloing, then we get The Other One. It has a classic start—Bill's tom-tom and Lesh's rumbling bass run—then Garcia and Lesh lay out counterpointing lines. There's a bit of a slowdown around the six-minute mark, but the improvising never lags, wonderful percolating invention.

After eight minutes, Garcia, Lesh, and Keith consider a return to the main theme, toying with it and then moving on. More propulsive twists and turns follow. They invent a sly variation on the main theme (12:56–) then flip it over and start driving it hard into the first verse (14:49). From there, it's an exploration of more dissonant ideas, wobbling wheels falling off the bus until wandering into Bach beautiful (18:20–).

Twenty-one minutes in, Garcia has a notion. As the band quiets, he repeats the introductory riff to Me & My Uncle until the band follows. Later, as Weir sings the final line about his uncle's dead ass, they blast back into The Other One, Keith going toe to toe with Garcia for awhile, a powerful sprint.

They return to Cryptical Envelopment and segue perfectly into Deal, with wonderful honky-tonk piano stylings.

A good to great night for Keith Godchaux, e.g., on Ramble On Rose his piano notes jangle like a janitor's keys (Garcia gets two solos). On Tennessee Jed (#7), during the "my dog he turned to me" line, Keith uncorks a twittering lick that ends with a top to bottom glissando (3:29–), a great moment.

October 1971 is perhaps fairly well represented in official releases (10/21/71, 10/22/71, 10/26/71, 10/31/71), but this evening's The Other One alone makes this performance worthy of similar attention.

Link to recordings

## 1973 ST. LOUIS, MO
# KIEL AUDITORIUM

The first of two nights here, great jamming in Eyes Of The World, Truckin' and The Other One.

Late in set one, Eyes Of The World makes a rare appearance (only six more would be played in the first frame). Garcia's initial soloing here is perky and articulate; he furnishes fast, slithering lines. After the seven-minute mark we get the bass solo. In the final minute, furious, frenzied jamming becomes the bells of Heaven ringing (14:50–) as they go from balls-out to ballad in thirty seconds. Among the best back halves of early '70s versions of Eyes.

The Truckin' outro jam has an exciting crescendo. By 8:30, the ride slows, with Lesh hitting harmonics and cymbals shimmering. A new jam emerges (11:10–); Lesh, Keith, and Bill form a jazz trio for a couple minutes until Garcia joins. They end somewhat dissonantly and yield the floor to Bill for a drum solo.

Lesh wakes the band from its slumber with his signature bass lick that starts The Other One. It's a twenty-two minute journey with some compelling improvisation; there's no sign of the Spanish lady until they turn it down to a low boil (5:56). Then things get weird, culminating in Garcia's Tasmanian devil's tornado of twisted tones (10:30).

Just after fifteen minutes, we hear Keith's repeating piano figure, then Garcia's Irish jig, and they pull themselves out of the interstellar hole they dug, racing towards the lily fields.

Link to recordings

 1977 DEKALB, IL

# NORTHERN ILLINOIS UNIVERSITY (NIU), CHICK EVANS FIELD HOUSE

On the opening Might As Well, during Garcia's final vocal chorus, you can hear that he's got some extra horsepower tonight. The concert includes everything from the unusual (a "Drums" segment slotted after Space and St. Stephen) to the sublime (Garcia's big moment during Bertha). This is one of the best performances of the Fall tour.

Set one closes with Let It Grow; the inside jam kicks off with Garcia's trademark, high-pitched warbling stutter (2:48). The "rise and fall" jam starts with soaring lead guitar phrases and propulsive drumming (4:08–) and later features more of those warblers (6:42; 9:06). The final "I am" jam begins with some relentless chording from Garcia.

Bertha starts set two; the solo has an initial four runs, swinging easy and melodic. After the bridge, Garcia goes nuts, hitting the heights at the start of the first run and ending it with a tsunami of swashbuckling chords; it's simply amazing (see 4/12/78 for a similarly scintillating stint on Bertha). Listen also for more of the delightful galloping drumwork from Bill and Mickey.

Good Lovin' follows. It's a song where Garcia's soloing over the years typically does not shine. Here, it's putty in his hands, mercurial and flying, even during a couple of the small fills behind Weir's vocals. Both of his two solo runs are fabulous, Bill and Mickey driving him to a wild peak at the end of the second.

In St. Stephen, amidst the jam, Garcia touches on the Beethovenesque theme (6:10–) that will become a masterpiece (1/22/78). The answer to The Answer Man is a Not Fade Away cadence courtesy of Bill and Mickey, but it morphs into a Drums section that Lesh soon joins, creating a trio for a couple of minutes.

There's more of Garcia's stratospheric soloing on Not Fade Away, plus some of the merry melodic stuff (5:55–). He invents a brand-new melody line that evokes St. Stephen's spirit. The drummers' upbeat pace suggests they'll drive straight into something like Sugar Magnolia (7:05–), but instead they slow it down masterfully, from a locomotive to a limp in less than thirty seconds.

Black Peter features a rare slide guitar solo and some fine work on the three-minute exit jam, Garcia repeating a classic descending blues figure in the final minute before a rough transition into Sugar Magnolia.

The Magnolia exit jam finds Garcia playing mostly all chords until a brief breakout at 5:15. There's a longish bit of mischief from Bill and Mickey before they launch a spectacular Sunshine Daydream with more of the impassioned vocals Weir has delivered most of the night.

"Thank ya'll very much for comin', good night." –PL

Deadbase X respondents ranked this performance tied for the eleventh best concert of the year, and voted Eyes Of The World sixth best all-time (a particularly popular performance among the Headyversion faithful, they rank both Black Peter and Might As Well best-ever, and vote many others here top ten all-time).

Link to recordings

## 1980 NEW YORK CITY, NY
# RADIO CITY MUSIC HALL

After a Tuesday night off, the first of the final three concerts here.

During the acoustic set, there's an unusual amount of banter, e.g., before and after The Race Is On ("this next one's dedicated to our surly and recalcitrant equipment boys" –BW).

The initial electric set is generally low-key. The guitars sound more professional than passionate on Feel Like A Stranger, Franklin's Tower, and Big River. Mickey and Bill do kick it up, but it doesn't help Garcia find his fifth gear until the set-closing Music Never Stopped.

That one has flashes of trilled chords from both Garcia and Weir towards the end of the inside jam, exciting stuff.

The last set has a good China Cat → Rider to begin. The transition jam starts subdued, but then Garcia reels off a series of interesting descending licks (5:20–). During the final I Know You Rider solo, we get warbles and more chord flourishes.

Post-Space, The Wheel's exit jam is short but takes an interesting turn; Garcia plays Lost Sailor-like notes (6:15) before running off into what could be a Playin' jam. Instead, we get Saint Of Circumstance, a rare placement for the song (it was only paired with something other than

Lost Sailor half a dozen times until 1986). Garcia hits the heights here, as the main jam builds to a raging peak.

Black Peter follows; there's some Jerry Garcia Band-like phrasing at the start of Garcia's inside solo, and a brilliant stuttering phrase in the exit jam (8:50–8:57), sparks flying.

Link to recordings

## 1985 ATLANTA, GA
## FOX THEATER

Set two opens with a blast from the past—Mississippi Half Step → Franklin's Tower—not played paired since 10/17/82. Franklin's itself was a rarity in 1985, performed just four times. The lengthy, unique Jam after Crazy Fingers is another highlight.

After an initial tuning section that is Space-quality, starting with a reverberating fun house, they unveil six songs in the first set. That's unusually short for this year, though each of them features extended jamming.

Set two starts with another minute or so of that unusually spacey tuning. Mississippi Half Step has a jaunty tempo, but the inside jam is tiny, just four runs (3:43–4:11), perhaps the shortest since they started the tune in Fall '72. The outro jam is similarly downsized, eight runs and they're on to Franklin's Tower, which also gets a Weight Watchers treatment.

Saint Of Circumstance has a great inside jam, Garcia does his whirling dervish act. After they end the song, they keep strumming—what's next?—and Garcia starts to pick out Crazy Fingers, their seventh of the year, the song's most prodigious season since 1976. But you'll hear lots of blown lyrics, including uncomfortable silences.

About two and a half minutes into the usual Crazy Fingers exit jam that becomes Spanish-flavored they take a breather, and Garcia noodles The Other One amidst sparse drumming. The jam sheds its skin a couple minutes later as they launch an all-new musical revue, fresh sounds that leave a smile and disappear into Drums.

Two minutes into Drums, we hear a thunderous session on The Beam from Mickey. Space begins with stormy skies, then quiets to a pin drop.

The Wheel is next, Garcia echoing through the hall, Brent's lines tracing his song Far From Me. Then we get The Other One that was hinted at pre-Drums. It's short but has strong, crunchy bass lines and Brent's free-association tinklings.

They close with Johnny B. Goode, plenty of fire there.

Encore: Brokedown Palace, tenth of fourteen they'll do this year, the most since 1980, and more than in any subsequent year. Some unique sentences come from Garcia's guitar at the start of his solo.

"Thank ya'll and good night." –BW

Link to recordings

# OCTOBER 30

1968 San Francisco, CA, The Matrix
(Mickey and the Heartbeats)

1970 Stony Brook, NY, The State University of New York
at Stony Brook, Gymnasium

1971 Cincinnati, OH, Taft Theatre

1972 Detroit, MI, Ford Auditorium

1973 St. Louis, MO, Kiel Auditorium

1977 Bloomington, IN, Indiana University, Assembly Hall

1980 New York City, NY, Radio City Music Hall

1983 San Rafael, CA, Marin County Veterans' Auditorium

1984 Berkeley, CA, Berkeley Community Theater

1990 London, England, Wembley Arena

1991 Oakland, CA, Oakland Coliseum

## 1968 SAN FRANCISCO, CA

# THE MATRIX

No Weir, no Pigpen. But plenty of jamming on Dark Star, St. Stephen, The Eleven, and The Other One. Jack Casady and Elvin Bishop join.

Link to recordings

## 1970 STONY BROOK, NY

# STATE UNIVERSITY OF NEW YORK AT STONY BROOK, GYMNASIUM

Two concerts on a Friday night. The early show features a Good Lovin' that segues into and out of Cumberland Blues. The late show has a rare opener, Smokestack Lightning.

Cold Rain And Snow begins the first frame. They fill the post-song dead air with a brief, jazzy/blues stroll, then launch Truckin'. It mostly moseys along at a laid-back pace. They'll play it again during the late show, the evening's only repeat.

Good Lovin' starts with Art Blakey-style samba drumming,* then there's a brief vocal section before they disappear into Drums. After Cumberland Blues we get the Good Lovin' jam. It's the kind of hard-edged, rock/R&B groove they usually laid down on Hard To Handle. Garcia finds a wonderful five-to-six note melodic figure (1:21) that creates a good 'ol Grateful Dead weave. Great stuff.

The late show starts with Smokestack Lightning; it's the last time they would open a set with it (they tried it four other times before this one). Garcia is on slide guitar for most of his solo.

"Hey, now, have no fear by the time we get finished playin' folks, it'll be November." (–BW)

On Dancin' In The Streets, the band breaks out into a short Tighten Up jam around the five-minute mark. Two minutes later, it sounds like just Garcia noodling over the drumming; Weir reenters around 8:20. It then slows, and Garcia's soloing becomes Dark Starish.

The St. Stephen inside jam kind of fizzles out and departs from the tune's thematic qualities. It's more like First There Is A Mountain until Weir and Garcia strike up the strong, two-chord toggle that leads back to the final verse.

The front end of Not Fade Away is short, but stick around for Garcia's stunning bend mid-solo (2:52–), a high jump of Olympic proportions. Goin' Down The Road starts low key, nearly folky. You get a sense they might be running out of gas, no soaring jam here. They briefly reprise Not Fade Away before closing with a Turn On Your Lovelight that stretches twenty-two minutes.

Originally ranked ninth best of 1970 by Deadbase respondents, it later slipped just outside their top ten. The next night is rated far higher.

Link to recordings

*See *Horace Silver Trio and Art Blakey—Sabu* (1955).

1971 CINCINNATI, OH

## TAFT THEATER

The second of three in a row here in Ohio. A standard collection of songs from their current repertoire, they save the biggest segment for last, a Not Fade Away → Goin' Down The Road closer that runs over twenty minutes.

A lush early Jack Straw (#8) is played later in set one, it has some solid piano from Keith, especially on the back half. His rockabilly stylings are upfront at the start of Big Railroad Blues, the piano shining through most of the evening.

In set two, Comes A Time (#7) bats third, an album-quality rendering. They add the "extra" verse—"When the words come out; like an angry stream..." (see also 11/7/71). Garcia gives the next-to-last "empty cup" line his best falsetto.

In Not Fade Away, after five minutes, they begin to explore new territory: Lesh with a descending bass line suggesting new chords; Bill with a roaming drum pattern; Garcia chasing his own tail; Weir beginning a new collection of chords. After seven minutes, Weir invents a new three-chord theme.

They give Goin' Down The Road a beautiful coda; you'll hear particularly pretty notes coming from Lesh's bass. They return to Not Fade Away, Weir singing without his usual sparring partner; Garcia fills in with lines that seem to reply.

Headyversion voters rank tonight's Comes A Time ninth best all-time.

Link to recordings

1972 DETROIT, MI

## FORD AUDITORIUM

This is their tenth gig in fourteen days, then they'll take a couple weeks off. They render twenty-seven tunes tonight in the hall that held Detroit's Symphony Orchestra for over thirty years.

The set one long-distance runners are Bird Song, China Cat → Rider, and the ever-lengthening Playing In The Band.

They start set two with Truckin' and go long, a sixteen-minute sojourn. The crowd claps along in time from the start. The exit jam rips, Garcia rocking hard and flinging distinct phrases everywhere. It slowly settles into a saunter. Around nine minutes in, you can hear where Nobody's Fault But Mine would fit right in.

Later in the jam, there's more great raunchy rock from Garcia (10:55–). Around the twelve-minute mark, they're still at it, Lesh roaming all over his fretboard, Weir slashing. Where to?

They return to the Truckin' vocals and the crowd again puts their hands together, prelude to another round of raucous jamming; there's seemingly no quit to this version. Wonderfully sustained.

They close with a rousing finish. Sugar Magnolia would suffice, their 24th song of the night, but they top off the finishing musical sundae with Goin' Down The Road and Not Fade Away, Weir in full throat on all three.

Encore: Uncle John's Band (not listed as the encore per se in Deadbase). Garcia's lines are melodic and even romantic, evoking feelings of happy and easy California living. The outro D minor jam is darker, already showing the potential for further exploration.

Very good '72.

Link to recordings

## 1973 ST. LOUIS, MO
# KIEL AUDITORIUM

The second of two here. Dark Star with a Mind Left Body Jam is the tip of the iceberg.

Here Comes Sunshine starts the concert—only the third time they opened with it (until the 1992 revival, i.e.,10/6/92). It quiets in the middle, offering you a chance to pick up on the Viola Lee Blues-style cadence. The set includes a China Cat → Rider with the "Feelin' Groovy" jam, and closes with a twenty-minute Playing In The Band.

Set two: Dark Star is the third number, Lesh begins with some truly innovative chord voicings. They give the main theme the slip after three minutes, soon drifting off (5:15–), Bill still giving it just enough forward motion to prevent a fall into Space.

And then, out of the blue, a brand-new stew with a unique, jazzy direction. Lesh starts another one of those (8:35–), perhaps channeling their inner Dave Brubeck, but it's clearly their own invention. The jam picks up steam around the eleven-minute mark, strange sounds coming from Weir's guitar, though that, too, recedes.

The Mind Left Body descending chords come a bit suddenly; the pattern is less well defined than on other versions. After a minute and a half, we get Garcia's slide guitar. They return to the Dark Star theme and then the first verse comes, sixteen minutes in.

Lesh's booming glissando leads them into a Space section that becomes pin-drop quiet. They return to jamming seven minutes later, mildly dissonant rather than stomach curdling. They forgo the second Dark Star verse and step into Stella Blue.

Link to recordings

## 1977 BLOOMINGTON, IN

# INDIANA UNIVERSITY, ASSEMBLY HALL

The night before (10/29/77) is a tough act to follow. The highlight here is an interesting, occasionally inspired Playing In The Band sandwich that closes set two.

The Playing In The Band jam has a complex texture, with great drumming throughout. You'll eventually hear Dark Star-like sounds coming from the lead guitar (9:07–). At the end, Garcia picks out the melody line from The Other One and runs with it.

He finds a distinctive, descending motif he repeats five times (1:20–) and drives to a stuttering peak around the three-minute mark, but there's no Lesh rumble up from the depths. Garcia and Keith repeat the main theme (4:40–), and the band vamps; are we just waiting around for Weir? It's a rolled-out red carpet for the bass player's classic introductory line, but he doesn't seem to be boarding this bus.

They again revisit the Other One theme (5:50–) and this time they seem to mean it. Regally raunchy effects engaged, Garcia blasts off, and the Spanish lady finally lays on them her rose (7:07).

The second jam also has some interesting lead guitar, culminating in a spinning, searing crescendoing peak (9:55–). After verse two, they quickly quiet and disappear into a relatively brief Drums.

Bill and Mickey begin to beat out a Native American pattern and The Wheel begins. The exit jam runs several minutes, a rarity on this song in later years. In the final minute, you can hear hints of Playing In The Band. Also rare is their decision to follow with another Garcia ballad, Wharf Rat (perhaps to balance Weir's Playin' → Other One couplet).

On Wharf Rat, the inside "true to you" jam (7:58–) features some fine soloing as well as boisterous banging from Bill and Mickey, along with Weir's clanging chords before the return to the final verse. There's another minute of jamming and a seamless return to Playing In The Band.

Link to recordings

## 1980 NEW YORK CITY, NY
# RADIO CITY MUSIC HALL

Set three is the ticket here, with forty-five minutes of music before Billy Cobham joins for Drums.

Shakedown Street opens that set; it's played just this once during the Radio City stand (and once at the prior Warfield run). They follow with Samson & Delilah, the final instrumental break turns up the heat. He's Gone is next, the last minute or so is just Garcia doing some high-speed noodling atop the drums.

Two minutes into the Drums section, the crowd cheers as Cobham joins. Around the seven-minute mark, one of the drummers begins to beat out

The Other One, a foreshadow. They toy with it again and stay loosely within that theme, eventually joined by Garcia.

There's no Space section, they simply go quiet before Lesh's rumbling bass line takes them into The Other One. The back half contains the more fervent jam.

After Wharf Rat, an amped-up Weir closes with Good Lovin', including the now regular nod to his former stablemate ("One more thing he used to say, you got to turn on your light, everybody's got one, you got to turn it on and leave it on.").

Link to recordings

## 1983 SAN RAFAEL, CA
# MARIN COUNTY VETERANS' AUDITORIUM

After a week off, the first of two here to end the Fall tour.

In set two, Ship Of Fools features especially strong singing from Garcia amidst a year sometimes vocally challenged. You'll hear a multitude of different and interesting vocal accents.

Amidst the Playing In The Band jam, Brent repeats Garcia's descending dancing lick note for note (6:31–6:40). After seven minutes, the jam settles a bit, then opens wide onto a Lost Sailor kind of canvas as they explore the great wide anywhere.

Space starts with Garcia's low-register, extraterrestrial conversation. Weir's fingerings steer Garcia into a slightly Spanish direction (see 10/20/83). Halfway in, it sounds like Garcia is ready for Truckin' but they keep wandering.

It becomes a quirky duet with Weir plus occasional tambourine and other percussion instruments until Garcia latches onto a speedy version of his starter Truckin' lick. They ride it for awhile before the more traditional start to the tune.

After a short exit jam, Weir drives them into Spoonful (#4) and quickly launches the lyrics. Garcia and Brent occasionally join the vocals.

Sugar Magnolia closes, it's high speed and rocked out.

Link to recordings

## 1984 BERKELEY, CA
# BERKELEY COMMUNITY THEATER

This is the third night of this stand with three more to come. The first set performance tends to outshine the second.

Dancin' In The Streets opens; it's their sixth and last rendition for the year. One of the better versions, Garcia hits some enticing high notes at the end of the jam. Brown Eyed Women appears mid-set; Garcia's hands are quick and clean, and he serves up sparkling notes on the final solo run. The band kicks into gear and makes a special push into the "ready to kill" lyric.

Cassidy has a tight jam, Garcia's guitar is blistering. Even Tennessee Jed sounds spry. Let It Grow closes set one with occasional supersonic streaks from the lead guitar, Lesh crunching away on bass.

Set two: there's a bit of a rough spot at the end of the Scarlet Begonias transition jam as they figure out how to enter Fire On The Mountain. Garcia repeats an upward, slicing five-note Fire pattern but they don't latch on to it, instead falling into an awkward stop that leaves each of them to find their own way in, though they do pull it together quickly.

At the end of Estimated Prophet, Garcia spins up a whirlwind (12:45–) while Weir tentatively pencils out Eyes-like chords. But after the drummers join, they can't seem to agree on the tempo. Garcia ultimately forces the issue by quickly starting the first verse. His first solo seems to run twice as fast as the rest of the band, an uncomfortable pace.

Space has some whale song (2:30–) and Garcia's Mr. Wizard-style incantations (5:40–) through a musical fog. Towards the end, amidst the mire, he starts to play with The Other One theme.

The band comes together powerfully just before the lily fields verse, Garcia hitting the heights, the likely highlight of the set. Stella Blue is next, his '84 voice holds up decently, along with a marvelous mercurial inside solo that ranges far and wide.

A decent performance and a fine example of the 1984 vintage, still in the shadow of the next night (10/31/84) that Deadbase respondents ranked just inside the top ten for the year.

Link to recordings

## 1990 LONDON, ENGLAND
# WEMBLEY ARENA

This is the first of three straight nights here that will end the European tour. Set one has a special section after Let It Grow and before they close with Bruce Hornsby's Valley Road (#2).

The Let It Grow jam is heavy on the faux James Bond theme, repeated ad nauseum. But Hornsby fortunately takes the final notes of the song and seamlessly works them into a wonderful something. A real treat for the audience, it's a piano-led improvisation that is going who knows where.

A minute and a half in, it's still Hornsby cooking up one theme after another, no Valley Road in sight. At one point, in the lower register, he repeats a rumbling figure that could have triggered Truckin'. After three minutes he hints at classic rock 'n' roll, a possible precursor to Promised Land, only to be left by the wayside, then revisited. Stunning.

He finally slows the train down, then blasts off into Valley Road a la Truckin'.

We hear no similar magic in set two, though there are bits and pieces of inspired play (e.g., Garcia's raindrops and rambling runs on Looks Like Rain, and Hornsby's sparkling fill after the "roll back down" lyric in Black Peter).

Link to recordings

## 1991 OAKLAND, CA
# OAKLAND COLISEUM

The third of four here. Set two has just three songs pre-Drums—Eyes Of The World, Estimated Prophet, Terrapin Station—and only three more after Space.

There's plenty of Hornsby as they tune up, hints of Louie, Louie, but they choose one of their own, Picasso Moon. It still sounds like a poor man's Hell In A Bucket.

Maggie's Farm has a Big River/Cumberland Blues feel, close cousins. They share the lead vocals in this order: Weir, Garcia, Hornsby, Vince, then Lesh.

Music Never Stopped closes, and Garcia begins his inside solo with an effect, nearly hornlike. He turns it off for the outro and it kind of slows the momentum. This has the newer arrangement where they hold the first of three chords longer. A set-closing anthem, this version has an underwhelming finish.

The set two Eyes Of The World is taken at an easy tempo. Hornsby gets the lead a couple of times on the inside jams, and he later gives a quick nod to The Girl From Ipanema (10:26–).

On Estimated Prophet, the Steely Dan-like lines sound better on piano than on synthed-up sax. Vince remains in the background until Weir's "na, na, na nahhh" chorus. The inside jam has a good group build. On the outro, Garcia goes to his flute effect, and Vince squawks sax.

Around the ten-minute mark, there's a big change in the jam. Garcia starts with the solo melody line from Terrapin Station and they kind of get stuck there, unable to find the tune's start where they park on the F chord. Hornsby helps them get there.

Terrapin Station gets a symphonic lift of sorts from Hornsby's piano. On the "not to master" inside jam, his parallel lines are interesting as Garcia gets quieter and quieter, perhaps signaling he's ready to make the turn.

Around 11:45, they leave the "whistle is screaming" jam behind and improvise for another four minutes. Hornsby takes the lead (14:45) a pretty, open jazz sound.

After Space, Hornsby starts The Other One and it sounds weak, a poor substitute for what is typically Weir's urgent rhythm guitar and Lesh's barreling bass. They go very quickly to verse one, after which Garcia's soloing lends it the familiar urgency. But even that well runs dry after a while, thankfully coming to a peak and getting on to the next verse.

Link to recordings

# OCTOBER 31

1966 San Francisco, CA, California Hall

1967 San Francisco, CA, Winterland Ballroom

1968 San Francisco, CA, The Matrix (Mickey and the Heartbeats) (no setlist, no recording)

1969 San Jose, CA, San Jose State College, Student Union, Loma Prieta Room

1970 Stony Brook, NY, The State University of New York at Stony Brook, Gymnasium

1971 Columbus, OH, Ohio Theater

1979 Uniondale, NY, Nassau Veterans Memorial Coliseum

1980 New York City, NY, Radio City Music Hall

1983 San Rafael, CA, Marin County Veterans' Auditorium

1984 Berkeley, CA, Berkeley Community Theater

1985 Columbia, SC, University of South Carolina, Coliseum Arena

1990 London, England, Wembley Arena

1991 Oakland, CA, Oakland Coliseum Arena

1969 SAN JOSE, CA

## SAN JOSE STATE COLLEGE, STUDENT UNION, LOMA PRIETA ROOM

We have twelve songs. The closing Turn On Your Lovelight clocks in at nearly thirty-two minutes.

Perhaps the most interesting piece is the China Cat Sunflower outro jam featuring Weir's lead, simmering organ sounds, and an extended journey before I Know You Rider (somewhat obscured by the quality of the recording).

The opening Casey Jones is still a work in progress, both the solo and drum parts are under construction. Three other *Workingman's Dead* tunes get a workout here.

Link to recordings

1970 STONY BROOK, NY

## THE STATE UNIVERSITY OF NEW YORK AT STONY BROOK, GYMNASIUM

The second of two nights here, early and late shows. They do two songs from *American Beauty* (the official release is still a month off) and three from *Workingman's Dead*. The rest ranges back to songs first played in 1966.

Notables from the early show include Till The Morning Comes, their fourth attempt. There would only be one more, and this version makes a good case for its retirement.

The following Hard To Handle is more up their alley. You'll hear a longer than usual jam, though without the brilliant, four-chord peak of, say, 4/29/71. China Cat → Rider is also solid.

Later in the set, there's an electric version of Dark Hollow. The only other plugged-in versions appear on 2/19/71 and 4/29/71.

They try Brokedown Palace (#7) next. Unlike the earlier song from *American Beauty*, the harmony vocals here generally shine.

Next up is Viola Lee Blues, on the shelf since 7/9/70. During the introductory vamp, it sounds like you can hear someone onstage offer a reminder on the words for the first verse. After five minutes, it moves along like a slow blues shuffle, a bit like Hard To Handle. Around 6:30, Garcia and the drummers pick up the pace. When Weir joins, the train begins to achieve Viola Lee speed.

And then, out of the blue, a moment of sublime alchemy. Right before your ears, the song magically transforms into Cumberland Blues. In its wake, Viola Lee vanishes into history (this rendition turned out to be their last).

They end Cumberland Blues and quickly pick up Uncle John's Band to close.

In set two, That's It For The Other One runs over twenty minutes; about a third of it is the drums section. Weir encounters a microphone issue right after he starts the lily fields verse: "…yoo hoo!…how 'bout now?…turn it up!"

They finish Cryptical Envelopment and wind it down to a note or two, clearing a path for a clean start to Cosmic Charlie. Still a regular in the repertoire, this is its first appearance in months. Weir appears to have some trouble with the lyrics after the "airplane" line ("Maybe I'll be back here, too…"). Garcia steps up on the next verses to provide some help.

"Hey, Pigpen, do you want to sing a song?"

Big Boss Man is next, Pigpen's second vocal of the set. He'll also drive Hard To Handle, their second performance of the song this evening, as well as Good Lovin'.

Link to recordings

### 1971 COLUMBUS, OH
## OHIO THEATER

The band delivers brilliant performances of Dark Star, Not Fade Away, and Goin' Down The Road. Garcia is a set-two savant.

Dark Star begins the second half, Garcia improvises melodically as they craft a delicate dreamscape. We hear some restatements of the main theme and notable peaks before the first verse, including a single-note stutter that sounds like a ringing bell (6:00–). Lesh's bass is often noticeably staccato in the early going, his notes on tiptoes.

After the vocal (7:18), Garcia goes on an exciting arpeggio run (9:08–). Lesh's popping bass (9:41–) soon triggers a new mad dash. Around 13:30, Garcia starts the two-chord shuffle that resembles the Tighten Up jam. Just as it begins to sound like they intend to leave it behind (15:42–), they extend it. There's another fantastic summit around 17:15, Garcia nailing the Tighten Up melody in the highest register of his guitar.

They finally slow the train after the nineteen-minute mark, quiet chromatic dissonant stumbling, then a couple of vibrating whirlpools. Amidst these choppy seas, Weir starts the chords for Sugar Magnolia.

As they bring the curtain down on Magnolia, Garcia picks out the first notes of St. Stephen. The inside jam takes awhile to get going until Lesh drives the two-chord stomp. Garcia then peaks and finds a wonderful seven-note motif before slamming his chords hard. Played far less this year, few would guess that this would be the last one for almost five years (6/9/76).

They roll it right into Not Fade Away, a dead ringer at the start for the version that appears on the Skull and Roses album (*Grateful Dead*) (see 4/5/71). The inside jam begins darker and minor, like a speedier Hard To Handle jam, though Garcia quickly switches back into the happier, major key mode. More great licks in the final minute lead to a fabulous, stunning, mesmerizing peak (6:52–), a Grateful Dead Hall of Fame kind of moment.

Goin' Down The Road Feelin' Bad has an exciting four-minute coda featuring an extended exploration of the two chords prominent in Cold Rain And Snow (E-A). They crank up the tempo to form a perfect platform for Garcia's fast filiagreed licks. It feels like it ends too soon when they take the jacked-up pace back into Not Fade Away.

Deadbase respondents ranked this Dark Star sixth best all-time, and best of the year by a wide margin (4/28/71 was next, with 2/18/71 right behind) (Headyversion voters also have it sixth, but behind 2/18/71).

Link to recordings

1979 UNIONDALE, NY

## NASSAU VETERANS MEMORIAL COLISEUM

A Halloween treat—China Cat → Rider is played for the second straight gig (10/28/79)—and a Halloween trick: they open the concert with it, something they haven't tried since 3/16/73.

It gets off to a shaky start. Garcia's initial vocals are tentative, but it finds its footing after a few minutes. The intro to I Know You Rider is long and interesting; Garcia repeats a truly loopy motif featuring a rainbow bend (1:30–). He and Brent join Weir's "sun will shine" verse.

Perhaps it wouldn't be Halloween without some chaos and fright, and there's plenty of that in the first set:

> "Hey folks! You know uh…the poor souls here at the front are not only getting crushed…but they are disrupting our electrical connections, and this will not do as you well know…" –PL

> "Well anyway, Happy Halloween. I would like to remind you all that Halloween is not a legal holiday." –BW

Six songs in, after Big River, we receive more incantations and admonitions:

> "We gotta ask you all to step back again…" –BW

> "It's terrible what's happening down in front here. Give us a break." –JG

They cool down the crowd with Althea (#8) and follow with two more new ones to end the set, Lost Sailor (#11) and Saint Of Circumstance (#7).

Set two has its own tricks and treats: just two songs post-Space, and Truckin' closes the concert (see 11/21/78). Plus Weir's continued banter: "It takes a heap of homin' to make a pigeon toed."

Shakedown Street opens, a great sound. The jam is plenty funky, Brent sending up sharp jabs of synth. Later in the main jam, Brent grabs the lead and takes a brief solo before they make the turn and head home.

On Passenger, Weir has some trouble with the first verse, Brent joining the lead vocals as Donna used to. Lesh crunches away, providing a fat bottom. Ramble On Rose features a one-of-a-kind solo, an unexpected fifth run quiet as a mouse. It provides room for a Brent solo, but it doesn't materialize.

Post-Space, Wharf Rat, the outro jam becomes frenetic, Garcia bending and dancing at the top of his fretboard (9:15–), fitting calisthenics for the coming transition into Truckin'.

The Truckin' finale is a sweet treat. The first crescendo (5:18–) starts quietly, Garcia noodling meekly on the descending three-chord figure. Amidst the following jam, if you were in the audience, you'd probably be wondering what they might transition into.

Around 7:40, Garcia finds a new melody that sounds like a '50s rock shuffle. What's this, another crescendo coming? It's actually Weir who suggests it first, then Garcia begins his run (8:44–), again quiet as a mouse deep into his rise.

Then all hell breaks loose. Trilled chords, machine gun Chuck Berry licks, over the top.

Encore: Johnny B. Goode. Close your eyes and hear the spirit of '71 on the final run.

Link to recordings

## RADIO CITY MUSIC HALL

Powerful spirits abound on this All Hallows' Eve, the end of the eight-concert Radio City run.

It's the most compelling start to an acoustic set this Fall: Heaven Help The Fool; Sage & Spirit (their first since 8/13/75); and Little Sadie (their first since 2/28/70). They would not play these three songs again.

"Well we're really havin' fun now!" –BW

All are well played, and many of the other set one songs are also strong. Soloing on acoustic guitar over mid- to up-tempo tunes can be challenging, but the jam in Bird Song is fluid and interesting, among the best versions on the tour. Cassidy is also well done.

The end of set three has the most surprising segue, from Space into Fire On The Mountain, as Fire was nearly always preceded by Scarlet Begonias at this time (twice fronted by Ollin Arageed during the Fall of 1978).

Stella Blue has a beautiful start to the outro jam, Garcia slowly caressing the strings, sensitive and tender lines. He makes several runs into the sky before a quick turn into Goin' Down The Road.

"We got one last chance to say goodnight to everybody…" –BW

Encore: Uncle John's Band.

Deadbase respondents have consistently ranked this concert the best of the year, by a wide margin.

Link to recordings

## 1983 SAN RAFAEL, CA
# MARIN COUNTY VETERANS' AUDITORIUM

Their final gig before the New Year's run of shows, they grace the crowd with yet another St. Stephen (10/11/83, 10/15/83) after a nearly five-year hiatus. There would be no more.

The best part of the performance includes the start of set two, with the opening Help On The Way establishing an energetic pace. After a bit of a hitch traversing the entrance into Slipknot!, we get a fairly raucous jam with layered builds, Garcia hitting a final peak around the four-minute mark. The high-spirited energy rolls into Franklin's Tower, a crisp rendition, Garcia bursting into bloom at 11:15. Strong.

The opening sequence of Space begins with some singing and percussion from Airto Moreira. From there, drums roll, Garcia soliloquies, bells ring, and runs of Saint Of Circumstance-like lines unfurl.

Then it takes a brand-new direction as Bill and Mickey break out into wild, dancing samba rhythms. It sounds like a Carnival celebration, far more Jam than Space. They wind it down to a pinpoint, and we hear the first notes of St. Stephen.

While any rendition of St. Stephen is likely to excite an audience, this is not a particularly scintillating version. The main jam is nothing special, and they stumble over some of the final lyrics. The following jam sounds better, but they quickly shut it down and enter Throwing Stones.

Encore: Revolution (#4).

Deadbase respondents have consistently ranked this performance in the top ten for the year, including second best in the Deadbase X survey.

Link to recordings

## 1984 BERKELEY, CA

# BERKELEY COMMUNITY THEATER

The fourth of six on this stand, they perform their first I Ain't Superstitious, and Weir transforms the closing One More Saturday Night into One More Halloween Night. Matt Kelly contributes solid harmonica on a handful of tunes.

They start with an energetic first set, with only one lower-tempo song (Ramble On Rose). Shakedown Street opens the show, a long, consistently perky and danceable version, but there are no fireworks. Big River bats third and has a nifty final run; Garcia's quick wrists, trills and rolls are on display.

On Minglewood Blues, Matt Kelly takes the first break with decent harmonica. Garcia leads the longer than usual middle section (perhaps the wait for his solo turn fired him up), and he delivers a bustling, inspired solo.

Scarcely missing a beat they pick up Big Railroad Blues, though the rhythm starts slightly out of sync. On the second break, Garcia starts the seventh run and kind of creates an opening for Kelly, but the harmonica player can't seem to hop onto the locomotive.

The front end of Lazy Lightnin' sounds a bit tentative; it's played for just the third time this year (it would be their last). Supplication is stronger (there would be one more of these, 5/22/93). The jam quiets around 9:30 before a lower-energy rendering of the final vocals. The last minute is also on simmer.

Set two has six songs before Drums. I Need A Miracle is served up like a late '50s stroll, Matt Kelly also appears here. The outro jam meanders, laying the low-key groundwork for I Ain't Superstitious. It's generally underwhelming, and the rhythm goes through at least a couple of odd tempo changes (you will likely enjoy the 1985 versions more). He's Gone puts them on friendlier, more familiar footing.

Drums starts with mood-enhancing percussion and soothing electronica. It ends with a heartbeat that fades into tom-tom rolls, a bicycle horn, and a generally odd soundorama (e.g., a baby doll's cries).

The final minute of Space has a Moorish flavor, and in the last twenty seconds Weir and Garcia play the Mind Left Body theme before launching Morning Dew.

Encore: Satisfaction (the second of two performed this year).

You will have a much different experience if you listen to the soundboard recording (this review was largely based on the less compelling audience tape). Deadbase respondents ranked this ninth best of the year (far behind 10/12/84).

Link to recordings


## 1985 COLUMBIA, SC

# UNIVERSITY OF SOUTH CAROLINA, COLISEUM ARENA

The band's Halloween spirit is in all its glory at their first (and only) appearance in The Palmetto State.

They open with several minutes of assorted strangeness, including wolf howls, ghoulish laughter, and Finiculì, Finiculà,* then three more minutes of additional Halloween oddities (Space?). They follow with their first Halloween Werewolves of London, then Music Never Stopped.

"Thank you and good evening music lovers." –BW

While waiting for the next one, we hear about thirty seconds worth of what might have been pilfered from Teddy Bears Picnic.**

Shakedown Street opens set two. Weir sings "just gotta poke around" in a falsetto right before the outro jam starts. Around 11:30, there's a neat little peak driven by Weir's lick.

Playing In The Band is next. The start of the jam inhabits a happy, major key (D-C-G) before diving below the surface into darker, murkier waters. Later, after speedy Garcia runs, it begins to run out of gas and make a seemingly natural entrance into Ship Of Fools. Garcia is in his somewhat charmingly gruff voice, giving fresh twists on some of the words: "…you know I, still might WARnnn a few-ew-ew…"

As they finish the song, the crowd cheers, and rising from the din we hear Weir's pinpointy notes and Garcia's scamperings. Where to?

About three minutes in, it's anybody's guess. There are some interesting rising patterns from Weir, then a percussion instrument ascends to the top. Garcia's notes occasionally hint at an Other One cadence. They keep the crowd guessing with counterpoint between Weir and Garcia (6:50–). After eight minutes it sounds more Space-like, free sounds, before tipping their cap to Drums.

Space actually has as much jamming in it as soundscape; at one point, they seem to be creating a new rock song in their laboratory. Dear Mr. Fantasy follows, just one of two songs post-Space.

An interesting performance, though outside the Deadbase respondents' top twenty.

Link to recordings

*Finiculì, Finiculà is a Neapolitan song composed in 1880 to commemorate the first funicular railway, i.e, cable cars, on Mount Vesuvius.

**Teddy Bears Picnic, Edison Symphony Orchestra (1908).

### 1990 LONDON, ENGLAND
## WEMBLEY ARENA

The middle night of three straight here, they start with an eleven-song first set, nearly eighty minutes of music. The selected songs are from the '70s but for Little Red Rooster and When I Paint My Masterpiece. No songs in either set are from the 1989 *Built To Last* album.

Help On The Way opens, and the segue into Slipknot! is well executed. We get a short but energetic jam there with an exit navigated without a hitch. Franklin's Tower features some good soloing in a couple of places.

Near the end of the set, we hear Bird Song. Amidst the jam and out of the blue we get a nice run from Hornsby (5:22–). Garcia switches to his flute effect (5:50–), then switches back to build to the first peak. Around 8:40, he begins strumming the now traditional two-chord seesaw. It builds and then the air goes out of it.

Set two: nearly all the songs are from deep in the catalog (All Along The Watchtower is the only '80s song).

Scarlet Begonias starts a bit draggy, and Garcia's voice is particularly rough here. In the transition jam, he goes to flute and finds an interesting sideways melody (7:14–), seven runs worth, then offers up a variation.

In the final minute of the jam, they sound lost, then Garcia begins to pick through the first five notes of a Fire On the Mountain motif that is a full step below where it's normally played (departing from the usual B to A, going instead from A to G). It doesn't seem to help his strained voice.

The first Fire break has steel drum sounds that clash more than complement, though Garcia does later get off some good runs. The second break starts with Hornsby alone, it's nice to hear him get more room. On the final break, Garcia again uncorks some good lines. They sign off with the Scarlet theme and pause before launching Truckin'.

Encore: they pull Werewolves of London out of the treasure chest for the first time in exactly five years (10/31/85).

Deadbase respondents rank this on the outer edge of their top fifteen for the year (1990 involves an apples to oranges comparison, e.g., this concert is a vote ahead of several March '90 performances played with Brent).

Link to recordings

## 1991 OAKLAND, CA
# OAKLAND COLISEUM ARENA

The fourth and final performance of this stand, they'd play one more concert (11/3/91) before the New Year's shows. Set two finishes their memorial to Bill Graham with a Dark Star encompassing Drums, Space, and a rap from Ken Kesey, plus Gary Duncan of Quicksilver Messenger Service on guitar.

Set two, four songs in, Spoonful ends spacey and they wander into Dark Star. The first verse comes before they reach the four-minute mark. Soon thereafter Kesey begins his rap: "I was in DC, and when I got the message I thought of two things: I thought of, my son going over a cliff and Bill Graham sendin' a thousand bucks…"

It clearly inspires the band, as the instrumental jam behind the words begins to surge. Kesey ends by reciting the e.e. cummings poem, "Buffalo Bill." The jam subsides and they bow to Drums.

A couple of minutes in, chimes, bells, and electronica take over, soon it's all dancing between left and right speaker channels. We hear the pounding of the skins around the eight-minute mark.

Space is digitalia bouncing around the room. Later, the guitars join, including Gary Duncan. A blues theme emerges, stomping like Smokestack Lightning might (13:00–). Then they return to Dark Star, and we hear verse two.

There's just a minute more of jamming before switching gears to do the Stones' The Last Time. Weir finishes with particularly high-spirited singing, seemingly channeling Jagger.

Standing On The Moon is next, there's probably not a dry eye in the crowd ("I'd rather be with you"). After Garcia's solo, pin-drop quiet, Weir strums Throwing Stones quietly to himself to begin the song. "On our own."

They close with Not Fade Away.

Encore: their twelfth (and final) Werewolves of London.

Link to recordings

# ACKNOWLEDGEMENTS

First and foremost, to the Grateful Dead, and to all the people who helped make their music possible, thank you.

Next, to the tapers, who in the early days sometimes risked civil if not criminal penalties to record the music before their exploits were officially allowed. A very special thanks to them for generously sharing the fruits of their considerable labors.

Thanks to Internet Archive (Archive.org) for making their repository available generally 24/7, and to all of the Archive's reviewers who took the time to share their two cents (and sometimes more) about each concert.

This effort would also have been near impossible without my copies of Deadbase (primarily V and X), the book of my dreams, and the one I wanted to write myself back in 1979. An amazing resource, for which I am forever grateful.

Setlists.net was a very helpful resource among other sources of setlist information. Thank you.

Last but not least, I would like to thank four friends—Steve McConnell, King Oscar I, Steve Fuhrman, and Bobby Scher—who read my initial email musings on these concerts, which got this whole thing started. Without their encouragement, this book would not exist (yes, it's all their fault). Thanks guys.

# APPENDIX

## Methodology

There is more art than science to many things, including Grateful Dead concerts. Many factors influence our impressions of music. Here are the methods to this book's madness.

### RECORDING QUALITY

What a difference a tape makes. Compare a hissy audience recording with a brilliant Walker-Scotton-Miller soundboard recording, and your opinion about the performance may change considerably.

But soundboards are not a panacea. Some are better than others. And sometimes the audience recording is far richer than any soundboard.

So in the interest of both art and science, I listened to more than one recording of a concert date (if available), typically sampling every audience and soundboard recording. Where a recording was not available on Archive.org, other online sources were used (e.g., YouTube).

## PLAYBACK DEVICES AND EFFECTS

Some recordings seem to blossom with more volume, while others need no assistance. Undoubtedly, higher-quality playback systems with equalization tools will alter the listening experience. But such technology is not readily available to all, and this book is intended to be of interest to both the audiophile as well as the listener still spinning TDK SA-C90's (we know you're out there).

For this collection of reviews, in the hopes of getting it just exactly perfect, the listening was conducted as a carefully controlled experiment. Each recording was experienced the same way: at roughly the same volume, without headphones, and through similar playback devices, with no changes for treble or bass, and no effects added.

Generally, listening occurred through the built-in speakers of a 2007, 24-inch desktop iMac, and later, a 2019, 27-inch iMac.

## RECORDING TYPE

Video corrupts, and all video corrupts absolutely. The ability to see the musicians' gestures—smiles, windmills, or downward catatonic stares—undoubtedly influences opinions regarding a performance. Emotions seep in.

Case in point: 4/12/78, a wonderful performance on audio, but completely irresistible on video as we gaze at Garcia's Grand Canyon grin on Bertha, or his windmills on Truckin' (see future volumes for a review of this concert).

Video recordings are inherently unfair for three reasons. One, we don't have videos for most of the 2,300+ Grateful Dead concerts. Two, the vast majority of videos that do exist are from the final ten years of the band's performance history. Three, many dedicated listeners' impressions were formed in an audio-only universe (when readers were polled by Deadbase in the 1990s, video recordings were scarce).

Thus, for purposes of this collection of reviews, I lashed myself to the audio mast so as to avoid, like Odysseus, the Sirens of live concert videos.

One disclaimer: video, where available, was sometimes investigated to fact-check other reviewers' comments and to cross-check this reviewer's hypotheses on certain esoterica, e.g., whether a particular riff was created by accordion or synthesizer.

## PERSONAL ATTENDANCE

There's a big difference between hearing music live and hearing a recording. And your experience at a live concert may vary greatly depending upon where you were located (first row? back of the balcony?) and many other subjective factors.

Given the vagaries of memory, none of these reviews is based upon remembrances of concerts past, only upon recent experience with the recordings.

## THE ELEMENT OF SURPRISE

Recordings have 20/20 hindsight. They know what songs are coming next. Yet fundamental to the power of Grateful Dead music is the element of surprise. Magical segues are usually more sublime when the outcome is unknown, a luxury usually not afforded when listening to a recording.

For example, looking at the setlist for 3/9/81, you'll see the band transitioned from Estimated Prophet into Uncle John's Band. But then you listen to it and realize that they could have gone anywhere. At the concert, the audience was suspended aloft into delicious anticipation, pleasantly if not passionately spellbound.

Accordingly, these reviews sometimes try to account for, and give weight to, this je ne sais quoi that we can only imagine, or that a listener may have witnessed in person.

## PERSONAL BIAS

Garcia famously stated that the people who like licorice really like licorice, and when it comes to Grateful Dead music listeners often like their licorice a certain way: with Pigpen; before Brent; before Vince; or in as many different permutations as Baskin-Robbins has flavors.

People are often predisposed to favor concerts based upon positive experiences they had while attending (try convincing someone that their very first show was a lousy performance).

Even authors bent on impartiality are prisoners of their own experience to some extent. Having come of ears in 1979, my own personal bias likely favors the late '70s (and the '70s generally) over any other time period.

Reviews in other books and forums typically reflect this kind of personal bias. If you love 1969 concerts, you are more likely to review them extensively, and to review them favorably.

As much as possible I've tried to nip that bias in the bud. One helpful tool was listening to concerts only by calendar date, forcing my head to traverse four decades of Grateful Dead performances on a weekly and sometimes daily basis.

APPENDIX                                        301

Despite the challenges and perhaps the inherent conflicts, it is still possible to put on the cloak of a neutral observer and employ impartial criteria to provide some guidance on what was happening musically.

Here are some of the criteria used here: creativity and imagination as expressed in melodically and/or harmonically compelling instrumental themes, phrases, motifs, and transitions; vocal clarity and invention; speed; power; song selection; length of songs; set arrangements; and perhaps that certain something that can't be put into words (to paraphrase what the judge said about pornography, you simply know it when you hear it).

## PERSPECTIVE

If you are well acquainted with, say, one hundred performances, there may be one concert or one song that you consider "the best ever." But become intimate with over a thousand concerts and your perspective is likely to change.

Consider Sugaree. There are many versions where Garcia is inventive and powerful. But then listen to 5/19/77. It will likely alter your perception on what constitutes a great performance of that song.

Some listeners who favor the '70s concerts have trouble with the '80s. But force those folks to listen to a string of '90s performances, then send them back to 1985, and a new sense of appreciation of the '80s may take root.

This book will give every fan, from novice to expert, a chance to shake up their respective Grateful Dead kaleidoscopes.

## APPLES AND ORANGES

The reviews here do not generally compare concerts across decades, for the same reason you shouldn't compare Babe Ruth with Hank Aaron. The Grateful Dead were a different band in the '70s than they were in the '80s (personnel, instruments, sound system, repertoire, etc.).

There are some people who believe that the band was simply no good after a certain date. The truth is, the band performed well and not well in every decade.

There are perhaps a select few performances that are widely admired across decades (e.g., 5/8/77). But many of those performances are also considered "overrated" (yes, Cornell was voted both "favorite tape" and "most overrated" by Deadbase X respondents).

## MYOPIA

Within a single concert, performance quality may vary. A review that does not mention performance errors does not mean that it was error-free. And a review that raves about the performances of certain songs does not necessarily bless every other song performed that night (although sometimes it does).

The focus in the pages you encounter here is generally upon particular performance highlights rather than lowlights.

## HISTORICAL DATA

Any references to "nth time played" or "nth version" are based on the currently available recordings. Here's an example: the famous 9/3/67 In The Midnight Hour (thirty-one minutes in length) may be referenced as "#8," but they may have played it many more times before that date. There are missing setlists and missing recordings, mostly affecting concerts performed from 1966 through 1970 (after that we have more complete data).

New recordings are occasionally discovered or made available which change our understanding, including the number of times a song has been played. As of this writing, In The Midnight Hour appears to have been played more times in 1985 (seven) than in 1966 (six). But when the next 1966 setlist or recording surfaces, it may no longer be true.

Historical research continues on whether the band performed on a certain date at a certain venue. I have tended to list concerts for which we have at least one published report, but not where the evidence consists solely of personal recollection. Sources consulted for this purpose included Deadbase 50 (particularly the updates) as well as various blogs.

In sum, this book is based upon data existing at the time of its composition and renders viewpoints that are, somewhat, prisoners of their time frame.

## MISCELLANEOUS FACTORS

Concerts were reviewed one calendar date at a time, from the band's earliest year (1965) to their final year (1995). Occasionally, one or more of the next day's concerts were reviewed before finishing the day at hand.

## ABBREVIATIONS, SHORTHAND AND TERMINOLOGY

You will sometimes see "AUD" for audience recording and "SBD" for soundboard recording. The terms "Matrix" and "Ultramatrix" are occasionally used with less precision.

Sometimes songs are referred to using shorthand (e.g., Baby Blue for It's All Over Baby Blue, Women Are Smarter for Man Smart, Woman Smarter, and UJB for Uncle John's Band). Versions of songs are often denoted parenthetically as "#5" rather than "their fifth."

Initials that appear next to quotes generally refer to band members or others appearing on stage ("–BG" = Bill Graham).

For each concert performance reviewed here, the ebook will display a link to the Archive.org recording with the then current most views; it is listed first and referred to as "main," i.e., main recording. Where reference is made to a particular moment in time (e.g., "3:59–"), this typically refers to the main recording.

Other links to additional recordings are listed to provide more illumination on the performance. In many cases, the less viewed recordings are a better listening experience than those with the more substantial following.

Most recording links are accompanied by a footnote with additional information about the recording, such as track list errors, audio quality, song length, and other items.

Names of individuals listed along with the recording link refer to people who taped, transferred, or were involved in some other capacity with the recording.

The annotation "no recording" indicates I found no Archive.org or YouTube recording, although a recording might exist in other databases or private collections.

# RESOURCES

## (A SELECTIVE BIBLIOGRAPHY)

### BLOGS

Grateful Dead Guide
   http://deadessays.blogspot.com/

Grateful Dead Sources
   http://deadsources.blogspot.com/

Lost Live Dead
   http://lostlivedead.blogspot.com/

### BOOKS

Jackson, Blair, *Garcia, An American Life* (1999).

Jackson, Blair, *Grateful Dead Gear* (2006).

Scott, John W., Dolgushkin, Mike, Nixon, Stu, *Deadbase V: The Complete Guide To Grateful Dead Song Lists* (1991).

Scott, John W., Dolgushkin, Mike, Nixon, Stu, *Deadbase X: The Complete Guide To Grateful Dead Song Lists* (1997).

Scott, John W., Nixon, Stu, Dolgushkin, Mike, *Deadbase 50: Celebrating 50 Years of the Grateful Dead* (2015).

## CONCERT REVIEWS

headyversion
   http://headyversion.com/

## DISCOGRAPHY

Grateful Dead Family Discography
   http://www.deaddisc.com/

Wikipedia
   https://en.wikipedia.org/wiki/Grateful_Dead_discography

## LYRICS

Grateful Dead Lyric And Song Finder
   https://www.whitegum.com/intro.htm

The Annotated Grateful Dead Lyrics
   http://artsites.ucsc.edu/gdead/agdl/gdhome.html

## ONLINE FORUMS

Archive.org
   https://archive.org/details/GratefulDead&tab=forum

Reddit
   https://www.reddit.com/r/gratefuldead/

## RECORDINGS

Dick's Picks
   https://en.wikipedia.org/wiki/Category:Dick%27s_Picks_albums

Dave's Picks
   https://en.wikipedia.org/wiki/Category:Dave%27s_Picks_albums

Internet Archive Archive.org

YouTube https://www.youtube.com/

## SETLISTS AND SONG LISTS

The Setlist Program
  Setlists.net

The Deadlists Project
  http://www.deadlists.com/default.asp

Deadtracks
  https://deadtracks.com/

Jerrybase
  https://jerrybase.com/

## VENUES

Jerry Garcia's Brokendown Palaces
  http://jerrygarciasbrokendownpalaces.blogspot.com/

## ADDITIONAL RESOURCES

Historical Weather Data
  https://www.wunderground.com/history

Newspapers, Periodicals
  https://gdsets.com/80articles/80articles.htm

Posters
  http://www.deadlists.com/posters/

Ticket Stubs
  https://gdsets.com/60tickets/60tickets.htm